"As a woman who has battled anorexia nervosa twice, and nearly died trying to be the kind of beautiful the world champions, I cannot recommend this book highly enough. Elisa Morgan speaks of a rare kind of love, an Abba kind of love, which reaches down into the heart of every single woman and comforts the little girl within: the one who longs to know she is seen and heard, and more than that—delighted in. *Hello, Beauty Full* is a must-have manual for every aching spirit longing to find its way home."

— EMILY T. WIERENGA

AUTHOR OF *MAKING IT HOME: FINDING MY WAY TO PEACE, IDENTITY, AND PURPOSE*

"In a time when women are bombarded with messages about who and what we should be, *Hello, Beauty Full* is a reminder of what is true. Reading this book acts as a recalibration. It prompts an introspection of how we are each uniquely created and a discovery of new aspects of God's handiwork through us. *Hello, Beauty Full* will help women everywhere better understand their God-spoken, God-designed selves."

— ALEXANDRA KUYKENDALL

SPECIALTY CONTENT EDITOR, MOPS INTERNATIONAL

AUTHOR OF *THE ARTIST'S DAUGHTER: A MEMOIR*

"As women we often fail to realize that by critiquing our design, we critique the God who has a divine purpose for every detail of who we are, inside and out. When we view ourselves through a constant lens of negativity, we limit our vision of the ways that God wants to work through our unique gifts, experiences, passion, and positions of influence. Elisa uses this book to challenge all women to expand our understanding of who we are and how God sees us and desires to use us to impact the world. A must-read for every woman!"

— CHRISTIE LOVE

FOUNDER AND EXECUTIVE DIRECTOR, LEADHER

D0369826

"Full-bodied and brave, Elisa Morgan's glorious exploration of beauty punches a big hole in the Enemy's lie that you, woman and man, aren't enough. Turns out God created in each of us his beautiful best. Thank you, strong Elisa, for this magnificent, powerful, take-no-prisoners reminder: I am beautiful. We all are. Here's real help for how to accept that truth and live in it."

—PATRICIA RAYBON

AWARD-WINNING AUTHOR OF *UNDIVIDED: A MUSLIM DAUGHTER, HER CHRISTIAN MOTHER, THEIR PATH TO PEACE*

"Elisa's words hum with a rich fullness as they challenge our assumptions and massage the truth of our beauty deep into our hearts. A *beauty full* book for women of all ages!"

—JESSIE MINASSIAN

RESIDENT "BIG SIS," LIFELOVEANDGOD.COM

AUTHOR OF *UNASHAMED: OVERCOMING THE SINS NO GIRL WANTS TO TALK ABOUT*

"*Hello, Beauty Full* is thoroughly enjoyable because of Elisa's wit, wisdom, and transparency. But it is the depth of the book that captured my soul. With every passage I felt myself in conversation with God. I learned much about myself and, better yet, what self-imposed obstacles were keeping me from moving forward in many areas of my life."

—LORI RHODES

FOUNDER, CHICKTIME, INC.

"Never has a topic been more timely, or its handling more timeless. Thank you, Elisa, for using your scars and your "sway" to awaken wonder in all of us at the beauty we've ignored."

—CONSTANCE RHODES

CEO, FINDING*BALANCE*, INC.

FOUNDER/AUTHOR, MORE THAN A NUMBER CAMPAIGN

PRAISE FOR *HELLO, BEAUTY FULL*

"*Hello, Beauty Full* captured me in the introduction . . . I laughed out loud, then moved to gulping deep with misty eyes, all within the first ninety pages! With piercing honesty and gentle humor, Elisa Morgan will bring you face-to-face with who you think you are but then will take you to who you truly can be. More than a book, it's a holy woo from the God who loved us first and knows us best. As you let the words sink in, you'll feel like you are sipping a cup with your best friend, carried away on a journey that begins with your eyes and ends with God's."

— SHERRY SURRATT
CEO AND PRESIDENT, MOPS INTERNATIONAL

"*Hello, Beauty Full* is a work that is a must-read for women of all ages! Elisa Morgan has produced another page-turner filled with vignettes from her own life while sharing Biblical truths in an open, honest manner. The exercises and questions offered after each chapter provide a much-needed pause to reflect and digest the important lessons skillfully woven throughout this volume. As the founder of an all-girl international ministry led by women, I know this book is sure to serve as a tool in their toolbox, offering a chance for a renewal of their minds and a filling of their hearts. Goodbye, Hiss, and plaudits to Miss Elisa!"

— PATTI GARIBAY
NATIONAL EXECUTIVE DIRECTOR, AMERICAN HERITAGE GIRLS

"Elisa's mastery of language, her experience with life's misery, and her acceptance of God's mystery have prepared her for ministry—ministry to us. If you, like me, have ever felt less-than, girlfriend, you have come to the right book. Elisa gets our shame, our pain, our insecurity and calls us into our God-given dignity. It's taken me a lifetime to learn what she's shouting out from the rooftop of liberty. Lean in and learn: beautiful can be not only our reality—it is our divine destiny!"

— PATSY CLAIRMONT
AUTHOR, *YOU ARE MORE THAN YOU KNOW*
FOUNDING SPEAKER, WOMEN OF FAITH

"In *Hello, Beauty Full* Elisa Morgan will turn your thinking upside-down on how to evaluate your worth, shake off your shame, embrace your scars, and use your influence. This book asks hard questions, presents options on long-revered opinions about the role of women in leadership, and challenges women to seek truth. Read this book. Share this book. Discuss this book. It is definitely worth your time!"

— CAROL KENT
SPEAKER AND AUTHOR OF *BECOMING*
A WOMAN OF INFLUENCE

"Every one of us has the tendency to compare our insides to other people's outsides. When we do that, we never measure up. We see ourselves through the skewed lens of our imperfections and we miss out on what God says about us. Elisa has given us a gift by revealing the beautiful way God sees us, even in the midst of our imperfections. Pick up this book, put God's lens of truth on your eyes, and see your incredible value today."

— JILL SAVAGE
CEO, HEARTS AT HOME
AUTHOR OF *NO MORE PERFECT MOMS*

"In *Hello, Beauty Full*, Elisa Morgan invites us to see ourselves the way God sees us and to live *loved* in our worlds. What better way to teach our daughters, sisters, and friends that they are *beauty full*, too, than by living in God's beauty ourselves?"

— JULIE CLINTON
PRESIDENT, EXTRAORDINARY WOMEN CONFERENCE

"As a longtime student of beauty's many faces and betrayals, I did not expect this when I opened Elisa's book: dog-eared pages, underlines, held breath, tears. I know no woman believes she is beautiful. But there's a good chance that *Hello, Beauty Full* can begin to end the war we are all waging against ourselves. This soldier may be finally ready to lay down her arms. Thank you, Elisa!"

— LESLIE LEYLAND FIELDS
AUTHOR OF *FORGIVING OUR FATHERS AND MOTHERS*

"She's done it again! Elisa Morgan has boldly opened wide her heart and empowered me to have the courage to look inside mine. Elisa reveals the truth about the sacredness of the love and beauty that lives in our heaps of messiness. With masterful storytelling, time-outs for practical assessment, and a rhythm that leads back to the fearful and wonderful essence in each of us, *Hello, Beauty Full* is *the* book every woman must read. Between the words on every page, healing happens. I encourage you to give your heart, mind, body, and soul the gift that God knows it deserves. I simply loved it."

—TAMI HEIM
PRESIDENT AND CEO, CHRISTIAN LEADERSHIP ALLIANCE

"My friend Elisa is one of the most 'beauty-full-of-life' people I've ever met! *Ever!* Her raw, authentic words speak to every woman who has stepped foot out of her house and into this world of vain comparisons. Elisa has hit a nerve . . . a nerve that needs a root canal filled with the Truths of this beauty-full book!"

—YVETTE MAHER
EXECUTIVE PASTOR, NEW LIFE CHURCH

"If I were to create a list of personal descriptors, I fear my paper would fill with far more criticisms than praise. Stubborn? Uh, yes. Impatient? I'm afraid so. Generous, affirming, forgiving? Not nearly often enough. And beautiful? No way. To a woman who sees herself through the thick and cloudy lenses of personal lack, Elisa Morgan wipes the glass clean. With a comforting mix of personal revelation and Biblical explanation, she helps each one of us exchange a distorted self-view for a divine one. We aren't mistakes needing to be fixed; we're beautiful daughters, already loved."

—MICHELE CUSHATT
SPEAKER AND AUTHOR OF *UNDONE: A STORY OF MAKING PEACE WITH AN UNEXPECTED LIFE*

hello,
BEAUTY
full

hello,
BEAUTY
full

Seeing Yourself as God Sees You

Elisa Morgan

W Publishing Group

AN IMPRINT OF THOMAS NELSON

Published in Nashville, Tennessee, by W Publishing Group, an imprint of Thomas Nelson.

Published in association with Alive Communications, Inc., 7680 Goddard Street, Suite 200, Colorado Springs, CO 80920. www.alivecommunications.com

Thomas Nelson titles may be purchased in bulk for educational, business, fund-raising, or sales promotional use. For information, please e-mail SpecialMarkets@ThomasNelson.com.

Any Internet addresses, phone numbers, or company or product information printed in this book are offered as a resource and are not intended in any way to be or to imply an endorsement by Thomas Nelson, nor does Thomas Nelson vouch for the existence, content, or services of these sites, phone numbers, companies, or products beyond the life of this book.

Unless otherwise noted, Scripture quotations are taken from the Holy Bible, New International Version`, NIV`. Copyright © 1973, 1978, 1984, 2011 by Biblica, Inc.` Used by permission of Zondervan. All rights reserved worldwide. www.zondervan.com. The "NIV" and "New International Version" are trademarks registered in the United States Patent and Trademark Office by Biblica, Inc.`

Scripture quotations marked NLT are taken from the *Holy Bible*, New Living Translation. © 1996, 2004, 2007, 2013 by Tyndale House Foundation. Used by permission of Tyndale House Publishers, Inc., Carol Stream, Illinois 60188. All rights reserved.

Scripture quotations marked THE MESSAGE are taken from *The Message*. Copyright © by Eugene H. Peterson 1993, 1994, 1995, 1996, 2000, 2001, 2002. Used by permission of Tyndale House Publishers, Inc.

ISBN 978-0-7180-3413-9 (e-book)

Library of Congress Cataloging-in-Publication Data

Morgan, Elisa, 1955-
 Hello, beauty full : seeing yourself as God sees you / Elisa Morgan.
  pages cm
 Includes bibliographical references.
 ISBN 978-0-8499-6489-3 (trade paper)
 1. Christian women--Religious life. 2. Beauty, Personal--Religious aspects--Christianity. 3. Self-perception in women. 4. Self-perception--Religious aspects--Christianity. I. Title.
 BV4527.M634 2015
 248.8'43--dc23

                         2015009293

Printed in the United States of America

15 16 17 18 19 RRD 10 9 8 7 6 5 4 3 2 1

To Eva and Hilary.
You are *beauty full*!

CONTENTS

HELLO, BEAUTIFUL!

I punched open my garage door to flat morning air. Gray. Overcast. The kind of sky that tells you to go back inside. But I'd committed to this walk, so off I went in my baggy sweat shorts and striped tank top. A frayed "Waffle House Regular" baseball cap covered my not-yet-washed hair. I was a vision for sure.

Pumping my arms and angling my hips in my best speed-walk-look-like-a-dork posture, I took off down my street toward the entrance to the open space behind our house. I dodged as a man with two giant Samoyeds passed from behind. Ever since being nearly devoured by one such dog, I've cowered around this breed.

I took in Colorado's Front Range Mountains bravely peeking out from the fog in the distance. Ahead a biker approached, slowing to make his own way around the dogs, which were now some distance in front of me. As he stood to pedal back to pace, covering the ground between us, our eyes met. Though we both wore dark glasses, I could tell he was looking straight at me, but from behind the safety of my shades, I didn't mind. He smiled and offered a quick, decisive nod. A bodily wink. Just as his bike passed me, he wolf-whistled and spoke: "Hello, beautiful."

Huh?

Who was he talking to? I looked quickly to my right and left. No one. But oh—he couldn't have meant me! Was he kidding? A sideways insult? Or maybe he was a creepy weirdo and would return to pounce!

I forced myself *not* to turn around fully to check him out, *not* to flinch, *not* to react. *Danger!* I counted *one-one-thousand . . . two-one-thousand . . . three-one-thousand . . .* up to five, then sneaked a peek over my shoulder. The biker was way down the path, his legs working rhythmically, putting more and more distance between us. I was utterly safe. So why was I so on edge? Why did my heart pound still?

"Hello, beautiful." Intentionally—now that I knew he was gone—I considered the meaning of such an utterance. He said I was beautiful. Me. Elisa. Ha! He couldn't see beneath my Waffle House hat to my unwashed hair. Behind my sunglasses to my tired and unmade eyes. Beneath my external to my grouchy and ungrateful heart. More to the point, within the walls of my being to my insecure soul. He couldn't see the ugly.

Yet he uttered these words to *me*. *"Hello, beautiful."* I found myself juggling them like hot potatoes—flinging them hand to hand, looking for a better place to set them, some spot more deserving than me.

My mind stopped at an odd but familiar exchange I'd often had with a former board member when I'd served as CEO of MOPS International. I came to call him a curmudgeon. That crusty, cantankerous word described him perfectly. He was simultaneously both a bit gruff and winsomely warm. Initially

I was scared of him: his prickly, pokey approach to topics; his croaky voice punctuating conversations with objections; his bushy eyebrows roller-coastering from arching to furrowing and back again as he made his points.

Yet as I grew familiar with Dennis over decades of serving together in nonprofit leadership, I grew to truly enjoy his wisdom. Perhaps most endearing was his surprising response to my everyday greeting.

Me: "Hello, Dennis. How are you?"

Dennis: "I'm gorgeous!"

Odd response, especially for a man. Yet his reply was always the same. Every time. Like Barbara Streisand inhabiting Fanny Brice in *Funny Girl*: "Hello, gorgeous!"

While at first his unexpected response left me off balance, eventually I became eager for his one-word rearrangement of my world.

"Hello. How are you?"

"Gorgeous!"

Had to *love* that.

Was the biker's greeting so much different? *"Hello, beautiful."*

A thought trickled through. Just a word: *receive.*

I listened—receptively—again. *"Hello, beautiful."* The greeting lingered, like butter on one of those steaming potatoes. The words dripped down the walls of my mind, working into my mood, staining the surface of my eyes so that my vision blurred just a bit in a lovely yellow hue. Everything looked so much prettier that way: glowing and happy.

Running the tongue of my soul over the syllables, I mouthed

the vowels and the consonants. They moistened. I swallowed. An ooze gave way and flowed through me. *"Hello, beautiful."*

They seemed true. Yet in the very next moment, ridiculous. *Receive.*

Why was it so hard for me to believe that someone thought I was beautiful? No, go further—why is it so hard to fathom that I *am* beautiful?

Because I'm just like 96 percent of the world's women who don't see themselves as beautiful. Yep, that's right: only 4 percent of women *around the world* consider themselves beautiful.[1] That's a *stunning* number! And this stat is up from the 2 percent reported a few years prior.[2]

In their "Real Beauty Sketches" campaign[3]—viewable on YouTube as one of the most viral video ads of all time[4]—Dove engaged an FBI-trained sketch artist to draw women, first based on their own self-perception and then based on that of a stranger. Imagine describing yourself to an artist behind you who can't see your face, and the artist drawing exactly what you describe. Then a stranger describes you to the artist, who draws a second portrait. Okay?

So guess what the results showed? The strangers' descriptions were regularly *more* traditionally attractive and similar to what the subjects actually looked like in real life. In fact, more than 54 percent of women globally (that translates to some 672 million!) agree that when it comes to how they look, they are their own worst beauty critics.[5] We women can see the beauty in another, but we don't get our own.

Know what else?

I did a bit of research myself—just the casual kind—inviting my Facebook friends to respond to an anonymous Survey Monkey link. Most of my friends there are female and followers of Christ. Only 11.1 percent saw themselves as beautiful.[6]

And hey, it's not just women who care about perceived beauty. In a worldwide study, 34 percent of male respondents rate their looks as very important to them. The response was 61 percent in South Africa, 55 percent in Brazil, and 53 percent in Russia—yet only 49 percent view themselves as sexy (which seems to be the major evidence of beauty to men).[7] More than four in five men (80.7 percent) talk in ways that promote anxiety about their body images by pointing out what they perceive as flaws. And 38 percent of men would give a year of their lives in exchange for perfect bodies.[8]

Hello. What's the matter with us? What's the deal with how we see ourselves—or more to the point, how we see the One who made us and how we think *he* sees us?

Beauty. Maybe we're messed up in how we're defining beauty. In part 2 we'll explore a whole new glossary on the term and how we *do* fit such a description. But for now, can I suggest that the definition of beauty we need to embrace is best captured not in some full-lipped, slender-figured-with-bumps-in-just-the-right-places, young-and-*gorgeous*-on-the-outside mirrored image but rather in how God made us—you and me—in his image? We are "fearfully and wonderfully made" (Psalm 139:14). Inside. Outside. Upside. Downside. All sides. Beauty—real beauty—is defined as God defines it: how he sees us and feels about us because of Jesus.

Full. And maybe, too, we interpret the *full* part of beautiful as "just a bit." An eense. A weense. We put only a toe into the bath of beauty we possess, as if we'll melt, or freeze frigid and break. God offers more than a toe. He invites us to splash *full* in the splendor of abundance.

Hello. Beauty. Full.

Now, you may have looked at the picture of me on the back cover of this book before you started reading. And you're thinking, *What does* she *know about not feeling beautiful? She looks okay to me—even put together. She can't possibly relate to what I'm experiencing.*

Can I be honest? I know I don't look horrific. I work pretty hard to look decent for a photo that will be on a book.

That's not my point.

My point is that I'm aware that when you look at my photo, you are making conclusions about who I am and what I struggle with and how I might relate to who you are and what you struggle with. That I'm like you, or I'm not.

Can I ask you for something? Can you try—baby steps!—to trust me? This book is not about what we look like. Well, maybe it is a bit. But just a bit. This book is about who we *are*. It's about learning to see who we really *are* and believing what we see in such a way that we are free to *be* who we are.

When the biker passed me and offered his two-word pronounce-ment, *"Hello, beautiful,"* I instinctively recoiled from this label. Such words, directed at *me*, seemed preposterous. Ridiculous. Me? I may look okay on the outside, but there's a world of ugly within.

I say, "I'll pray!" and I don't.

I forget about the suffering in the world, even after I've seen suffering up close and personal. And then I go ahead and buy another purse, pair of shoes, trinket for my home.

I wake up in the middle of the night and worry.

I think I'm better than others when my life goes well, even though I know full well that I'm not.

I eat too many Doritos. I drink too much wine. I watch too many episodes of *The Bachelor* (and *The Bachelorette*).

I assume I'm the only one.

The only lonely one.

The only depressed one.

The only one who doesn't know the answers.

The only one who feels like a failure.

The only one who is nervous when she meets others and would rather stay home than go out and be friendly.

I don't like my body.

I like some people more than others—a lot more than others.

I pretend to be interested when I'm not.

I'm jealous when someone's life goes better than mine.

I want to just stay in bed on some days.

I snap and get really irritated at my husband and act like a b****. Oh mercy. I nearly wrote it.

I want my kids to like me and each other and be happy more

than I want them to grow up and be healthy adults. Not all the time, but enough that they notice and find me annoying—which, of course, I am in such moments.

I'm *ugly*. At least, there are plenty of ugly parts of me.

"Hello, beautiful"? Ha!

But as that stranger disappeared down the path and I stepped farther and farther into the solitude of my walk, the words lingered. There was something so wholly *true* in the statement that I couldn't seem to trash it. The words rolled over and into me, a definition of my being provided by my Maker.

Hello. Beauty. Full.

A pronouncement over my self and my soul that needed to be received and not rejected. To reject would have been—would still be—what? Disobedient? Foolish? Rude? Wrong?

Hello.

Beauty.

Full.

What if hearing and *receiving* these words—bowing my head under God's pronouncement of the beauty of my being—is the life work God has called me to?

Some words I read a while back from Brennan Manning's classic book, *The Ragamuffin Gospel*, seeped up into my thoughts. They had puzzled me in the moment, but now they formed with clarity. Manning quoted a 1677 prophecy to a thirty-four-year-old widow in Lynn, Massachusetts. God's words to her way back then—and maybe to me in this moment? "More pleasing to Me than all your prayers, works, and penances is that you would believe I love you."[9]

Hello.

Beauty.

Full.

God loves me. What if I love him back by letting him love me? By believing what he says about me? By seeing myself the way he sees me—beautiful? And then by living beautifully?

Hello.

Beauty.

Full.

The words didn't change me that day. They still haven't changed me totally. But they have begun their work in my soul, and each day they lead me a bit further into the "me" my Maker originally created. The "me" he had in mind all along. The "me" I already am in him.

I may think ugly thoughts and feel ugly feelings and do ugly things, but to God, I *am* filled with beauty and therefore beauty full. He holds out these words and calls me to receive them, knowing that when I see myself the way he sees me, I will be free to be who he made me to be and to live the life he made me to live.

I'm pretty sure I'm not the only one who pushes away God's pronouncement of personal value. Likely you do too. Likely you embrace the ugly and discard the beauty in yourself. And likely you feel incredibly inadequate, stuck, and even alone.

Want out? Want more? Want to see yourself the way God sees you?

Here's what we need to know in order to live the lives we were made to live: God loves us. He wants us to see ourselves the way he sees us: beauty full. We struggle with embracing such a thing. But the truth is, when we don't embrace how God sees us, we don't embrace God. We miss out on the very lives he created us to enjoy—and *died* to make sure we could experience. When we do embrace how God sees us—beauty full—we are freed to live loved, and in so doing, we love God back.

The path ahead won't be super easy. I'm pretty sure it'll take a while to get from here to there, and most likely there won't be some strange biker dude wolf-whistling a reminder at every step.

But God's here. And he sees us the way he imagined you and I would be. He's holding up the mirror of his Word in our world to remind us so we can keep clear and focused on what's real. So we can see ourselves the way he sees us. So we can love him back by letting him love us.

Hello. Beauty. Full.

Yes, I am.

And yes, you are.

part one

HELLO

Seeing Yourself the Way God Does

The whole concept of *hello* implies discovery. The word is British in origin and was originally an expression of surprise. *Hullo!*[1] With the invention of the telephone in the 1800s, the word was used to discover if someone was actually on the other end of the line.[2] *Hello? Anyone there?*

Hello is openness.

Hello is an invitation.

Hello is a movement toward discovery.

So here's where we begin: with *hello*, with discovery. We need to figure out what's the matter with us—with how we see ourselves and others and our world. With how we see God and think he sees us.

Because something is wrong when our response to "Hello! How are you?" isn't "Gorgeous!" or "Beautiful!" but instead is "Uhhhh...?" Something is wrong when 96 percent of us don't believe we—created by an all-powerful God in his image—are beautiful.

Let's discover how we get stuck and don't believe God, so that we can begin to see what God sees from his perspective.

one

THE HISS

Stop connecting with your darkness. Connect with the beauty of My risen life within you. You were on My heart eons before I created the galaxies and scattered a trillion suns across the void. I personally designed you and take great pleasure in the work of My hands.

—Pamela Reeve[1]

I hurled the phone across the kitchen, where it banged against the wall just below the oven and clattered to the floor in pieces. Gathering my weary heart, I crossed to fetch it, bending to note the gash in the Sheetrock where the phone had made contact. Ugh. The plastic notches wouldn't snap back in place, leaving random, unhooked wires and doobobs. And I was left with no ability to fix the conversation I'd just botched. I laid the phone on the counter and covered it with a dish towel for the moment. Mercy.

The phone hurling had come with good reason. My ministry-minded husband and ministry-minded me found our tidy world shattering. Our family of two beautiful teens was coming undone through an unexpected expectancy, substance abuse, and this, that, and the other unimaginable ordeal. Pain. Pain. Pain.

When a phone call came with more unraveling news, I came undone as well, and the phone went flying. It certainly wasn't the first time I'd launched leftover turmoil far out and away. Oh, no—frustrated flinging was familiar to me from times far back in my tumultuous childhood.

Like a certain Halloween night as a teen growing up in Houston. Looking back, I still can't see into my motivation. I'm not sure where I got the eggs—or for heaven's sake, why I thought it would be cool to hurl them here and there.

What I do remember is my hula girl costume, my finger on the doorbell, my body darting back down the front walk to hide behind some bushes, the door opening, and then my arm arching—launching a raw egg through the opening. *Splat!* It hit the target of the entryway, creating an artwork of egg yolk on the avocado-and-cream flocked wallpaper. I can still see the stunned look of the owner's face—first shock, then confusion, then anger. My trick-or-treating companion in crime (really just "trick" in this circumstance) rose from her hiding spot, and we took off, praying our costumes would sufficiently conceal our identities.

When I consider the "less-than" moments in my life, this one usually starts the list. The list is long. Other teen follies follow: smoking down at the bayou, sneaking champagne at a wedding reception and having to be carried home by my date, slipping a lipstick into my purse at the mall, riding atop a friend's car hood at youth group, shoving my drunk mother in the door-way to get her out of my face. There are adult infractions, when surely I should have been more mature: Slamming the refrigerator door—over and over again until the shelf arms broke and glass jars rattled onto the floor. Ignoring an inconvenient need in a coworker. Yelling at my husband. And my kids. And God.

Throwing the phone across the room after ending that exasperating call.

Of course there are many more failings. Rather than trot out all the ugliness, let me just admit it here: I've messed up. I've sinned. Let me make that present tense. I mess up. I sin.

And like everybody else, I cover up. I grab whatever fig-leafed excuse I can reach and put it in place over my mess. I tighten the drawstring on my grass hula skirt and flee the scene. I cover plastic phone parts with a dish towel and slide to the kitchen floor. And then I try to function as if I'm okay, confident, whole, *loved*, when I truly don't believe I am. Because I know what's underneath the cover-up. I know what's still stinkily *there*.

Enter: The Hiss

From the time he was about three, my grandson Marcus would spend the night every other weekend or so. One bedtime, cuddled with him in his race-car bed in his upstairs "Marcus room," I reached for a book a friend had suggested to me in my newish grandmothering role: *The Jesus Storybook Bible* by Sally Lloyd-Jones. There was something so whimsically engaging about the art and the layout that I had tucked it up on the bedside table to open more fully with Marcus.

I picked it up. It began,

> God wrote, "I love you"—he wrote it in the sky, and on the earth, and under the sea. He wrote his message everywhere! Because God created everything in his world to reflect him like a mirror—to show us what he is like, to help us know him, to make our hearts sing.
>
> The way a kitten chases her tail. The way red poppies grow wild. The way a dolphin swims.[2]

I was liking this. Marcus was too. We exchanged a smile, and I continued on through the story of creation.

> "Hello stars!" God said. "Hello sun! Hello moon!" And whizzing into the darkness came fiery globes, spinning around and around—whirling orange and purple and golden planets. "You're good," God said. And they were.[3]

Marcus was now wide awake and eager for more of this story. I glanced at the clock—getting late—then turned the page to "The terrible lie." Curious, I caved and continued.

> Adam and Eve lived happily together in their beautiful new home. And everything was perfect—for a while.
>
> Until the day when everything went wrong.
>
> God had a horrible enemy. His name was Satan. . . . He

wanted to stop God's plan, stop this love story, right there. So he disguised himself as a snake and waited in the garden. . . .

As soon as the snake saw his chance, he slithered silently up to Eve. "Does God really love you?" the serpent whispered. "If he does, why won't he let you eat the nice, juicy, delicious fruit? Poor you, perhaps God doesn't want you to be happy."

The snake's words hissed into her ears and sunk down deep into her heart, like poison. *Does God love me?* Eve wondered. Suddenly she didn't know any more. . . .

And a terrible lie came into the world. It would never leave. It would live on in every human heart, whispering to every one of God's children, "God doesn't love me."[4]

I read on a bit farther—who wants to go to sleep on *that* note? Then I marked our place, closed the book, and snuggle-prayed with Marcus until he fell asleep.

Downstairs, in my own bed, the Hiss stung my ears. Today it stings still. *God doesn't love me.*

To look at me today, you wouldn't think I would dance to this beat. I seem confident in who I am and clear about what God has placed me on this planet to accomplish. But beneath my smiling greeting, my kind offer, my outstretched arms, the lie slithers. It undoes my doing. It pricks my confidence. It erases my perception of beauty and whizzes a lie of *ugly* in place of the twinkly hope that maybe I could somehow be okay, even loved.

God knows this. He knows that I've heard the Hiss—*God does not love me*—and that I have believed it. That because I've believed the Hiss, I do not see myself the way God sees me. He understands that this great lie is what beckons me in and out of each day, away from him and all he offers.

"How are you?" someone asks.

Inside, my reply gurgles up: *Ugly*. In response, I reach for the fig-leaf covering and offer some words: "Oh, pretty good." A throw rug over a stain on the carpet.

Made in the image of God—*beautiful*—Adam and Eve were naked and unashamed before the lie was told and received. They heard the Hiss, believed the lie into disobedience, and became ashamed. With their hearts twisted by untruth and their trust diminished by doubt, their beauty became defiled. Ugly entered. "They sewed fig leaves together and made coverings for themselves" (Genesis 3:7). A temporary covering. A fragile facade. The best they could manage with their limited abilities.

In their book *The Cure*, John Lynch, Bruce McNicol, and Bill Thrall pronounced, "Here is the lie, in two parts: We do not see God as He is, and we do not see ourselves as we are."[5]

Exactly.

The Hiss continues in each of us as the curse is handed down: pain in childbirth, confusion in the relationship between husband and wife, sweaty work for survival, eventual death (Genesis 3:14–19). Our failures followed by God's rejection—forever. We're sentenced with a kind of vision impairment: our inability to see ourselves the way God sees us.

And then the tender irony: God created clothes for his embarrassed image bearers. After the lie's original Hiss—*God does not love you*—God bent and fashioned the first fashion: "The Lord God made garments of skin for Adam and his wife and clothed them" (Genesis 3:21). Isn't that stunning? God himself clothes his wayward ones. The God who X-ray visions through any cover-up we concoct yields to our need to hide and covers us himself.

Although the fall caused clear consequences of separation for Adam and Eve, God's love for them does not change. What changes at the fall is their *understanding* of God's love and their ability to grasp that he still sees them as good, even beautiful. As does ours.

The Hiss's Legacy

We experience a multisensory depravity. The Hiss in our ears distorts our vision of who God is and how he sees us, and therefore, how we see ourselves.

As Brennan Manning observed, we make Adam and Eve our role models,[6] leaning into some world-made, society-formed version of beauty for our value. When we find ourselves lacking, we christen ourselves "un." Unwanted. Unimportant. Unvalued. Unnecessary. Unloved. Unclothed. Unworthy. Uneverything. We run for cover, coverings of our own making, trusting such masks to provide safety, even a kind of self-salvation. In her book *Daring Greatly,* shame expert Brené Brown called this "armoring up."[7] Problem is, armor can protect, shield, and cover, but it also cuts us off from real acceptance and love.

Beauty, as God defines it, is pre-fall and post-resurrection. God created us in his image. Male and female he created us. And along with everything else God made, he saw us and said we were good. *Very* good (Genesis 1:31). Then came the great lie. And we believed it. So God gave his Son—his one and only Son—that believing in *him*, we might be restored to God. God wraps the bleeding body of his Son over our "un-ness" and restores us to his original design, inviting us to see ourselves once again as good—just as he always has. Beautiful. "Redemption," as theologian Jerry Sittser put it, is "becom[ing] who we already are in Christ."[8]

In my most stripped-down, honest moments, I realize that I rarely *really* believe God's pronouncement of "good" over me. More quickly I tune my ears in to the Hiss. How did this ancient murmur become so powerful in my modern life? How does the volume of white-noise falsity grow so loud?

I think back to a moment with my father when I was five years old. He had beckoned me aboard his knees in his cushy, white armchair in our den. Holding my shoulders and peering into my eyes, he said, "Elisa, I've decided I don't love your mother anymore. We're getting a divorce." *Hissssss! God does not love you!*

The Hiss continued as I faced the harsh truth that my mother couldn't be stable for me, as she herself was addicted to alcohol and needed me to be stable for her. Answering the call of her alarm by getting her up in the morning and off to work, supervising my younger brother's whereabouts, cleaning cat vomit hairballs off the knotty pine planks of our breakfast room floor, Ajax-ing ashtrays . . . *Hissssss! God does not love you!*

Again, when my boyfriend of six years and I ended our

relationship on the steps of engagement. *God does not love you!* Again, when my husband and I waited nearly five years—forever—for our first child through adoption. *God does not love you!* When a trusted coworker betrayed me. *God does not love you!* When my adolescent children stepped into choices I had prayerfully directed them to avoid, and endured life-changing consequences. *God does not love you!*

The Hiss has not always come as a result of the choices of others. There are plenty of moments when it slithers through mistakes of my own making: a shrill scream at my husband, a gruff—even mean—moment of mothering, a slip in sharing with another what was not my story to share. Why am I so bad? Why do I do such things? Why doesn't God help me make better choices? And even when I try oh-so-hard to be good and do good, why doesn't God intervene to prevent bad things from happening to me? Why am I so ugly and so not beautiful? *God does not love you!*

I look at my life. I look at my choices throughout my *hisssstory.* I look at myself, and I believe the Hiss: *God does not love me!*

Can you hear the Hiss in your ears? Accusing. Doubting. Ruining. The great lie hisses its way through oh-so-many layers of our living! When we pull back the covers, pad into the bathroom, and see ourselves in the mirror. When we catch glimpses of our reflections while entering a store. When checking the rearview mirror while backing out of a parking place. When staring blankly at our images in kitchen windows, washing dinner dishes. When brushing our teeth before heading back to bed in the late hours. We believe the Hiss: *God does not love you!*

And in believing the Hiss instead of God, we wound not only ourselves but him as well.

Like all of humankind, I face a choice. Will I choose the Hiss? *God does not love you!* Or will I choose my God? *I love you, Elisa!*

The Hiss leaves me with no option but self-salvation. And because of my unavoidable list of failures, I know well that this is not an option at all. Like Sister Miriam, a novitiate in Mark Salzman's novel, *Lying Awake*, who is trying so very hard to be good enough to be a nun, I discover, "We all have to try to become holy on our own, and fail, before we can approach God with humility."[9]

Silencing the Hiss

God offers a promise of something else entirely: a permanent way out and ahead. Such a stunning turn of events offers full-time hope. Fourteenth-century mystic Julian of Norwich wrote, "Our courteous Lord does not want his servants to despair because they fall often and grievously; for our falling does not hinder him in loving us."[10] Modern-day contemplative Sarah Young ratcheted this thought into an invitation from God: "Don't let feelings of failure weigh you down. Instead, try to see yourself as I see you."[11]

This is the promise that God created me to live under: God loves me, and because he loves me, he sees me as beautiful. Period. Can I believe him so that he can fulfill this pre-fall and post-resurrection promise in my life?

Rather than abandoning me to act sinful, God invites me into acting saved. Rather than leaving me indentured as a slave to shame, God releases me to unfettered freedom. Rather than only rescuing me from how I've been wounded, God heals me whole, as if the evil never occurred.

I reach for my list, topped by my phone throwing and Halloween hula girl egg-chucking escapade and continuing through the years with failure after failure—both mine and those done to me—added until the edges curl up with age. I tear it up. First horizontally, then vertically, then again and again until the pieces are tiny snowflakes that I fling into the wind. But it's a new flinging this time: toward freedom.

And you? Where is your list of "ugly"? What will you believe about it and the "you" it represents?

God loves me, and God loves you. Just as we are. And God sees us as he made us: good. Beautiful. Beauty full.

What will you choose? How will you orient your days? Whose words will you trust regarding who you are and what you're doing here? How will you define your value—your *beauty*? By the Hiss or by your God?

Becoming Beauty Full You

1. Can You Hear the Hiss?
God does not love you! Sit with this lie, and then invite God into it. When have you felt most unloved by God? What does God say about you, even in that ugly moment? Let his words of truth silence the Hiss. *God loves you.* He made you in his image. Fearfully and wonderfully he made you. And he looks at you and says, "*You* are good."

2. The List
Make a list of your failures: those you've done and those done to you. Line after line, consider the mess. Then take it and tear it, first horizontally, then vertically, then again and again until the pieces are tiny snowflakes. Fling them into the wind and feel the freedom.

3. She Said—He Said
Reconsider who says what about you, and what you are attuning yourself to, through this essay by Karen Schelhaas. Are you listening to the Hiss ("She Said") or to God ("He Said")? What would you write in your own two columns?

She's persuasive, pushy even. I keep thinking I can unfriend her, but she insists I keep her around. She speaks in ways that are familiar to me. I listen.

She says I'm a mediocre spouse, that the sum of my failures is a giant slap in the face of Christian marriage. This is a hole I've dug, and there is no new, higher ground.

He says, "See, I am doing a new thing! Now it springs up; do you not perceive it? I am making a way in the desert, and streams in the wasteland" (Isaiah 43:19). He takes broken, hard things and makes them soft, even new.

She says if my kids or friends act out or lose control, I should back away, especially in public. She whispers that my good name is all I've got.

He says, "Carry each other's burdens, and in this way you will fulfill the law of Christ" (Galatians 6:2). Love is messy, embarrassing, and complicated. He invites me to dive in, head first, unashamed.

The swellings from four babies, the zippered abdomen riddled with scars covering what's left of my angry intestines, the National Geographic breasts. She says I'm disfigured, grotesque even. I must hide myself.

He says, "They will be called oaks of righteousness, a planting of the Lord for the display of his splendor" (Isaiah 61:3). I am a beautifully scarred tree, still swaying for His glory.

She says to clamp down my mouth, to keep words of wisdom birthed from heartache and struggle concealed, because nobody really wants to hear them. My experiences yield little; my failures mar my credibility.

He says, "For it is God who works in you to will and to act according to his good purpose. Pearls of wisdom don't come cheap, and when unveiled can be exquisite jewels of hope for others.

She is shame, and He . . . is not. May I have the courage to pry her out of my life and instead receive God's voice, trusting that He makes beauty from ashes. I have a choice.[12]

two

NOT ME!

Even before God made the world, He chose us.
We really are preapproved. He loved us before
we stepped one foot on the planet. Before God
created Mount Everest, the Great Barrier Reef,
or Niagara Falls—before He even sent the globe
spinning on its axis—He decided to love us, in
Christ. We are preapproved.

So, the question is: Are you ready to believe it?

—Jennifer Dukes Lee[1]

Throughout the writing process for my memoir, *The Beauty of Broken*, I clattered at the keyboard with a cringe in my heart. A wincing wondering at what the response might be once the thing was typeset, bound, covered in color and image, and stacked on bookstore shelves for all to see. *The Beauty of Broken: My Story and Likely Yours Too.* Ugh. My story. Honest and transparent and not take-back-able. The story I'd been stewarding under my loyal leader/mom/wife being for over a decade, now revealed for friends and strangers alike to read and *know*.

Or not. Maybe it wouldn't even get that far. Maybe the book would be stocked in ones and twos and set tentatively spine out so that a consumer would have to hunt, as for a random item listed in a scavenger hunt. (#4: Find a book published by an author with the last name Morgan in the year 2013.)

But even the thought of one person reading the story I had never publicly told rattled me to my core. A single word filtered through my thinking, clawing for permanent residence: *disfavor*.

I had spent most of my life—child and adult—seeking favor. I had bought the formula that being a good girl would bring me good. Obedience + obedience + obedience = blessing. At least the way most of us define *blessing*. Turns out that this formula is pretty much bunk. I'm glad to finally discover the freedom that comes with releasing the mythology that there is such a thing as a perfect family, a perfect way to live, and a perfect life that is blessed. Gradually I've come to see the beauty of broken. God brings a kind of beauty in my broken that has nothing to do with my obedience or failure but rather with the reality of his purposeful presence in *all* of life. And his ability to redeem—to make it *my* beauty as well, not just his.

So while I don't think I really ran after favor as my number one goal, I sniffed out where it might lie and skunked along in pursuit of its spoils *as* I obeyed, *as* I sought out the next right decision, *as* I lived and loved and led. It came: favor. I attracted it much like the kid who brings regular-size bags of M&M'S—not the snack-sized ones—for the after-game treat. People liked me. They pretty much always have.

The very thought of pouring out a story where I wasn't the

heroine and, in fact, could be seen as villainous—disobedient and ugly and proud and *yuck*—left my heart clutched cold. How would readers respond if they knew my teen daughter had become pregnant, my son had struggled with addiction, while I was president of MOPS International? Surely they would see my children's choices as my fault! (I myself did in many moments.) What about all the other layers of my family story—both my original and my second families? The divorce and alcoholism, the legal issues, the coming-out-of-the-closet revelations, the inmate-visitation-room ponderings? I pictured readers, both friends and strangers, reading along, and then—*bam!*—gasping, slamming the book shut, and hurling it across the room in horror at . . . *me*!

Disfavor. Not being liked. Disrespected. Disapproved. Unpopular.

I'd spent most of my life avoiding my fear of this word: *disfavor*, and I didn't want it now. When asked how I thought the book would be received by others and what my prayers for it were, I shared this word—*disfavor*—and prayed for protection.

Before the first radio interview for the book, I prayed that God would somehow connect my story to the stories of those listening. Within the first forty-five seconds of the chat, the host's voice caught in her throat, and she said she had always felt so alone in her brokenness before she read the book. I stammered through the next fifteen minutes in stunned acceptance. As I began to speak the message elsewhere—to my church at four services one weekend, to women's retreats, and at fund-raising events and various dinners and lunches and teas—slowly . . .

certainly . . . clearly, a swell of resonance began to rise. People were deeply encouraged by discovering they were not alone in their brokenness. Elisa is broken! We are all broken! God loves the broken! And God can use the broken—sometimes even more effectively *because* they are broken!

Disfavor? It never happened. Surprisingly, in its place came comfort and freedom and peace. Who knew?

So why did I fear disfavor? Beneath my sincerest efforts to tell the story that God has written in my life—to share the beauty of broken—has been an honest and undeniable sense of call from God's heart to mine: *Share what I've shown you.* In obedience and trust, I did just that. I wrote. I shared. *My* story—not the stories of my children or my husband or my sister or my brother or my parents. No, I wrote my story, the one I'm responsible for sharing.

If God was calling me forward to speak, why was I afraid? I touch some possible reasons.

On the one hand, my story reveals that formulas don't work. Specifically, the formula I had invested in—that so many of us invest in—that if we know and love Jesus and raise our families to know and love him, then—*bing!*—we'll raise happy and whole families filled with folks who know and love Jesus. But that result is by no means guaranteed. That's disappointing, and not a popular proposition. Aren't we all more comfy with formulas that guarantee a desired outcome?

Then there's the reality that my story reveals that I did some stuff poorly. Bad Elisa. In the process of my breaking, I discovered I was proud and judgmental and thought I had answers I didn't have, that nobody really has. I overfunctioned as a parent, assuming that I was responsible for the choices of my children and defined by their outcomes.

Both reasons resonate and hold elements of reality. Of course I feared disfavor. Who would favor such a woman?

I tug at the strings of these thoughts and create an even bigger knot. I did life wrong + I'm bad = disfavor. Ooohhh: I'm still trying to *earn* God's love. And the appreciation of others.

The tangle tightens. I slide my musings this way and that until I discover another undeniable source for my fear of disfavor: I don't actually believe that God is favorable toward me. I don't believe what he says about me is true.

I'm stuck. Even though I know better, I'm still listening to the Hiss. Whether silently whispering or clobbering with accusation, the Hiss sends me seeking something I already have: favor. It takes different forms in my days.

Hiss #1: Not Me! I'm the One Big Exception to God's Love

Does God really love you? Sure, he loves the world and people everywhere, but how do you know he loves you?

Somehow I've decided I'm the one big exception. I'm too much. Too bad. Too broken. Too much of a mess. Too needy. Too ugly. Oh, I recite in obedience that Jesus died for the forgiveness of our sins, but I live like he died for everyone *but* me. Because I don't *really* believe he loves me. Or sees me as beautiful.

I reread my own words, written over and over in these very pages. God loves us. He thinks we are gorgeous creatures. And when we fall and break, when we are less than he made us to be, he makes our brokenness beautiful. I begin to see that I feared disfavor—still do at times—because I don't completely believe that what God says about me is true. And in not believing, I sin. I push God's love away as if it weren't love. I say God isn't who he says he is and doesn't see me the way he says he sees me. I disbelieve.

Once again, I know I'm not the only one.

But it's so hard, isn't it, to *really* believe that God loves us, that he sees us as beautiful. We ebb and flow. Over the years of my walk with Jesus, I've become aware of the ongoing discovery of who he is, in and with who I am at the moment. I once heard that "becoming a Christian is one big *yes* and a thousand uh-huhs." Someone else commented that we give all of what we know about ourselves to all we know about God.

Embracing God's view as our own is such a long process, one that changes us as we journey.

Hiss #2: Not Me! I'm Afraid of God's Love

Does God really love you? Is it safe to let him love you? What might happen to you if you yield control to him?

When I keep listening to the Hiss, I discover that it's often *fear* that unknowingly drives me to hiding from God and his view of me. Fear of being misunderstood. Fear of failing. Fear of not being enough. Fear of being known—really known—and maybe not liked. Fear of being out of control.

In the words of William Paul Young, author of *The Shack*, the root of sin is "independence. It is declaring ourselves the arbiters of right versus wrong, rather than being in a dependent relationship."[2] He suggested that this sin of independence manifests itself as "the inability to trust, or the need for control. . . . We create systems in order to not have to trust someone. And systems largely are an expression of our fear, which desires to control so that we have some certainty."[3]

Jesus healed a demon-possessed man in Luke 8. (A similar story is also recorded by Matthew and Mark.) The story reveals that *many* demons had gone into this man—so many that he called himself Legion, but not too many for Jesus to deal with. He cast the demons into a herd of pigs and sent them off a cliff into a lake. *Boom!* Gone. The response of the town that had witnessed the insanity and then the restoration of a soul to himself? Fear! Sure, the locals were freaked at Jesus' authority over demons—crazy stuff. But they were also afraid that Jesus would mess with their way of living. Pigs were their livelihood, and he had just sent some two thousand off a cliff.[4] Mark 5:17 tells us that the people "began to plead with Jesus to leave their region." Luke raises the curtain to reveal the motivation behind these pleas. Fear. Fear. Fear. "Then all the people of the region of the Gerasenes asked Jesus to leave them, because they were overcome with fear. So he got into the boat and left" (Luke 8:37).

I'm no different. I'm so overcome with fear of Jesus, and

how he might love me and change my world, that I pretty much push him out of my life. It's as if I ask him to leave, to get into a boat without me. I struggle with trust. I take back control. In so doing, I decide I can provide for myself better than Jesus can. I believe I can protect myself better than Jesus can. I determine I can guide myself better than Jesus can.

But I'm wrong again. I'm listening to the Hiss. The most common command in Scripture is "Fear not," because it takes God speaking, "Fear not . . . Fear not . . . Fear not . . ." over and over and over in our ears to eventually hush the Hiss.

Hiss #3: Not Me! I Have Too Many Doubts About God's Love

Does God really love you? How can you know for sure?

Wouldn't it be *awesome* if God literally appeared in the mirror right beside us each day and reminded us that we are beautiful? That beauty is about more than the way we look—but that even our looks are beautiful to him? God is just so . . . intangible. Quiet. Far off. The Hiss is so loud and seemingly more ever-present.

Way back as a teenager, I joined the apostle Paul in asking his question from Romans 8:35, "Who shall separate us from the love of Christ? Shall trouble or hardship or persecution or famine or nakedness or danger or sword?" I entered a laboratory experiment with the verse, acting out each element in my day as it occurred. Trouble? God's love appeared clear and real when I failed a test in high school. Hardship? God's love intercepted my mother's inability to be present for me and need for me to be present for her. Persecution? God reminded me of his love when my parents didn't understand or value my faith. Famine? Well, I never actually *starved*, but I sensed God serving up his love in those moments when my stomach demanded food.

And then one morning, preposterously, while I showered and prepared for my day, God reminded me that nakedness also could not separate me from his love. Even there, in my raw and vulnerable state of nakedness, God saw me and loved me. Something shifted inside my heart.

"For I am convinced that neither death nor life, neither angels nor demons, neither the present nor the future, nor any powers, neither height nor depth, nor anything else in all creation, will be able to separate us from the love of God that is in Christ Jesus our Lord" (Romans 8:38–39). What can separate me from the love of God in Christ Jesus? Nothing.

Do I believe this?

Decades after my Romans 8 experiment, I ping-pong my way through this reality in life: Nothing can separate me from the love of God in Christ Jesus—or can it? Not death—or can it? Not life—or can it? Not trouble—or can it? Not hardship—or can it? Exactly how much does God love me? Exactly how much of me does God love, so that nothing can separate me from his love?

Just as Thomas, as his name Didymus (meaning "twin") suggests, housed both doubt and belief in his being, I reach out my hand for the hole in Jesus' side, begging him, "Convince me of your love!" "Tell me again!" "What is it about me that makes you love me—no matter what?"

In the silence that follows I hear nothing. Instead, I feel my hand dragged to a wound, healed but still very real in his risen being, proof of his brokenness: "By his wounds we are healed" (Isaiah 53:5).

He loves me not because of me but because of himself. Rather than offering just words to convince me, Jesus demonstrates his love in action. He died to love me, and love me he will. No matter what.

Jesus said to Nicodemus, "Very truly I tell you, no one can see the kingdom of God unless they are born again" (John 3:3). Jesus told Thomas, "Because you have seen me, you have believed" (John 20:29). Believing and seeing go together. Seeing leads to believing, which leads to more seeing and more believing.

I see.

I believe.

I see more.

I believe more.

Doubt is ever-present in the life of a believer. The Hiss remains, but when we tune our ears away from the Hiss and toward God's voice, our more accurate hearing results in more accurate seeing. We hear better. We see more—and therefore believe more.

Hiss #4: Not Me! I'm Not Good Enough to Deserve God's Love

Does God really love you? There are so many others who are much better than you! You can never measure up!

When I first saw Nancy Blackwell's cooler-than-cool track shoes—white leather sneakers accented with black patent leather

Adidas-style stripes—striding her into sixth-grade English class, I knew I *had* to have a pair.

It didn't matter that my family didn't have the kind of money the Blackwells had. Well, it sort of mattered. I actually felt pretty guilty as I began my pleas to my unmarried, working mother for a pair. But this urge within me would not be silenced.

The shoes promised—what, exactly? Coolness like Nancy's coolness? Just-a-little-better-than-others status?

My mother was pretty good at figuring out when I was just angling out of a whim and when I seemed to need something for the formation of my identity. In her estimation, the track shoes fell in the latter category. So one afternoon after school, she drove me to Sears, and giddy with excitement, I walked out of the mall—literally—in my own pair of black-and-white track shoes.

For a full week, the shoes never left my feet. They walked me to the bus and through the halls of junior high. I would pump my crossed leg in math and then switch legs, admiring their sleek profile. After school they arched above my back as I lay stomach-down on my bed, yakking to a friend on the phone. In the evening the cat snuggled up against them on the couch as I watched *Bonanza*, and on Wednesday night they traveled to youth group, where I displayed them on my outstretched legs in our Bible study circle.

The next Monday, Nancy wore another pair of shoes to English class. Magenta patent leather Mary Janes. I stared at her feet, and then at the now seemingly "out" track shoes on my feet, and sighed. Not enough. Again.

Not-enoughness plops us on a hamster wheel of comparison

that pushes us into competition and wears us weary. How am I doing compared to *her*? What about *him*? What do I need to compete in order to get ahead of *her*? Of *him*?

I'm pretty sure this isn't the daily focus God desires for me, or for any of us. I'm pretty sure he doesn't evaluate *me* based on *her* or *him*, but rather on Jesus.

Ann Voskamp whacks me upside the head to stop such comparison and competition. (Okay, Ann never whacks anyone anywhere with anything. She's just way too gentle for such a thing. But at times her words sure have grabbed me by the shirt and held me up to stare straight into Jesus' eyes.) She wrote of those who compare and compete,

> If your life looks like a mess—*to them*—they whip out a measuring stick and feel confident of their own worthiness.
>
> If your life looks like a monument—*to them*—they whip out a measuring stick—and start cutting you down for their own empowerment. . . .
>
> Walk through life with a measuring stick—and your eyes get so small you never see God.[5]

Or his true view of me.

We can get completely contorted on the concept of having to be *better than* in order to be valued and loved. We categorize people into columns of "winners" (who have power) and "losers" (who don't), because we think there's only so much power. If we don't get it, someone else will, and we'll miss out.

Jesus unwinds our thinking and carries us to the cross to reevaluate our assumptions. The night before his crucifixion, Jesus washed his disciples' feet, surely a "loser" action in a world where only slaves offered such a service. But look at how John offers the assumption—the rationale—behind Jesus' gesture:

> Jesus knew that the Father had put all things under his power, and that he had come from God and was returning to God; *so* he got up from the meal, took off his outer clothing, and wrapped a towel around his waist. After that, he poured water into a basin and began to wash his disciples' feet, drying them with the towel that was wrapped around him. (John 13:3–5, emphasis added)

Note the word *so*! Jesus knew he had *all* power and therefore was free to serve above or below our understanding of power. *So* he bends to serve. And then he goes on to tell us to do the same thing—to model our lives after his living: "Now that I, your Lord and Teacher, have washed your feet, you also should wash one another's feet. I have set you an example that you should do as I have done for you" (John 13:14–15).

We see power as win/lose, a zero-sum game where someone gets it and someone loses it. But Jesus had—has—*all* power, so he could stoop to serve so others could have power too. In Jesus' economy, power is win/win/win. We all win in Jesus: You. Me. God's purposes in our world.

God's Words About Us

Now what? As editor David A. Zimmerman wrote, describing the theme of Patty Kirk's book, *The Easy Burden of Pleasing God,* "The work that God expects of us is nothing more and nothing less than to believe in Jesus, the One God Sent."[6]

To believe means to accept as true. To live differently because it's true. To share with others because it's true.

So what, exactly, *does* God say about us and about how he sees us?

He knows us—through and through.

> You have searched me, LORD,
>> and you know me.
> You know when I sit and when I rise;
>> you perceive my thoughts from afar.
> You discern my going out and my lying down;
>> you are familiar with all my ways.
> Before a word is on my tongue
>> You, LORD, know it completely. (Psalm 139:1–4)

Before I formed you in the womb I knew you. (Jeremiah 1:5)

He made us—and says we are wonderful.

> For you created my inmost being;
>> you knit me together in my mother's womb.
> I praise you because I am fearfully and wonderfully made;

your works are wonderful,

I know that full well. (Psalm 139:13–14)

He chose us—to bear fruit.

I chose you and appointed you so that you might go and bear fruit—fruit that will last. (John 15:16)

He loves us—just the way we are.

As the Father has loved me, so have I loved you. (John 15:9)

But God demonstrates his own love for us in this: While we were still sinners, Christ died for us. (Romans 5:8)

He stays with us—even though he's gone from the earth.

As I was with Moses, so I will be with you; I will never leave you nor forsake you. (Joshua 1:5)

Though my father and mother forsake me,

the LORD will receive me. (Psalm 27:10)

He plans for us—and the plans are good.

"For I know the plans I have for you," declares the LORD, "plans to prosper you and not to harm you, plans to give you hope and a future." (Jeremiah 29:11)

And we know that in all things God works for the good of those who love him, who have been called according to his purpose. (Romans 8:28)

He favors us—approving us with care and kindness.

Therefore, there is now no condemnation for those who are in Christ Jesus. (Romans 8:1)

I still struggle. At times I wonder if I'm the one big exception to God's love. I see and believe—and believe and see—God's love for me, but I doubt and question it as well. I poke at the prospect of his unending favor, exploring from a safe distance, wrapping control around me like a cozy muffler in a chilly breeze. I'm not done with this lesson of learning to believe that what God says about me is true. If I were done, I'd be dead. But I am further convinced, and in that further conviction, I am more whole and therefore more able to receive and be who he says I am: *favored.*

As are you.

Becoming Beauty Full You

1. Romans 8:35
Take some time to "enter" each element of Romans 8:35 for yourself:

"Who shall separate us from the love of Christ? Shall trouble or hardship or persecution or famine or nakedness or danger or sword?" Go ahead—try it on.

2. See and Believe—Believe and See
In what areas have you been able to see God at work and then been more able to believe that what he says about you is true? In what ways has believing that what God says

is true helped you see him working in your life and your world?

3. Fear Not
Quiet yourself to think, and then fill in the blanks with those things you fear:

Fear not _____.
Fear not _____.
Fear not _____.
Fear not _____.
Fear not _____.

Invite Jesus into your fear to sit right there with you.

three

SHEDDING SHAME

Those who look to him are radiant;
their faces are never covered with shame.

—Psalm 34:5

I walked into the women's restroom, finding it yawningly empty. Nice. My feet crossed the eighties-style, lumpy, rose tile, and I raised my hand to push open the matching pink stall door. Why did they use this color so much? It looks like old-lady flesh.

My movements halted as I suddenly realized I wasn't alone after all. The stall wasn't empty. Hunched back next to the toilet, about the height of the flushing handle, a little girl crouched with her bone-thin arms raised above her head, her hands covering her face. Her blue-gray dress was stained. White socks had lost their grip on her ankles, their exhausted elastic hanging above her scuffed, black patent leather shoes.

I stepped back from the stall while propping the door open with my hand. I needed a better look, but a bit more distant. I didn't want to intrude, and yet I wondered if she needed my help.

Her fine, brown hair was staticky about her shoulders in

stringy tangles. Dirty fingernails dug into her cheeks before she lowered her hands to reveal a Dalmatian coat of grime across her face. She looked up and locked eyes with me, and I sucked in my breath under the penetration of her gaze.

There was an immediate familiarity between us. Though she remained stiffly in place, her eyes galloped to me, devouring the distance and diving into my presence. I felt a push-pull: an attraction and also a need to turn and run. My body stiffened to escape while also folding to the ground to form a tuffet for her hug.

I gathered myself and rose back to my feet. In the seeing and being seen, I realized I *did* know this little girl. I knew her well, though I'd never seen her in this state of need up close and personal. She was *me*. Dirty. Skinny. Bruised. Needy. Broken.

While this moment never actually happened in real life, the envisioning of it came true enough. During a season of multiple layers of therapy for my mind and soul, "Little Elisa" began to appear to me, bringing me the gift of my own brokenness in Rainbow Brite color. I honestly can't remember if she first appeared to me in a dream or in a daydream or maybe even in a conversation with a counselor, but appear she did, leaving an indentation on my try-so-hard-to-be-happy heart.

The thing is, even with all the energy I invested in therapy to heal the mess of my first broken family (broken first through alcoholism and divorce and then through distance and loneliness), I never once discovered that I was molested or beaten or truly abandoned. I was never left hungry, forgotten at school, or locked in a closet. Why did Little Elisa appear to me in this form?

Why did she wear the garb of grimy shame when she presented herself to me? And what did she want and need?

Many of us—*most* of us—are well acquainted with shame. We wear shame as a second skin. It's the go-to garment in our closets, hanging happily alongside both our fat sweatpants and our skinny jeans, perma-pressed and ready to wear.

In church services, we go forward to freedom and shed the scales of our sin, only to watch them involuntarily reappear like a mutant identity when we shut our car doors for the drive home.

Shame is epidemic! It's well documented that women uniquely struggle under the shadow of shame, both real and imagined. Victims of abuse—sexual, domestic, and other versions—struggle with shame. Postabortion studies reveal high levels of shame. Those who experience financial failure, marriage breakups, infertility, and wayward children share common experiences of shame. Seventy percent of women feel depressed and ashamed after looking at a fashion magazine for three minutes.[1] In her March 2012 TED talk viewed by millions, Dr. Brené Brown—today's expert on shame—commented, "Shame, for women, is this web of unobtainable, conflicting, competing expectations about who we're supposed to be. And it's a straight-jacket."[2]

No kidding! With our arms tied about us, we wrestle with humiliation and guilt and shame, pretzeling our souls in a futile attempt to get free.

Humiliation comes from what happens to you. We can't help what happens to us. But we can process it and find freedom from the results.

Guilt grows over what you do. We have a very real need for confession of our all-too-real failings. We've done wrong, but Jesus died for our sinfulness: "If we confess our sins, he is faithful and just and will forgive us our sins and purify us from all unrighteousness" (1 John 1:9). Done deal. Right?

Nope—at least not for most of us. *Shame* goes deeper, to who you are. Like the annoying static cling of plastic wrap, grabbing onto everything we don't want it to grab, shame sticks and re-sticks to us, no matter how far away we fling it.

Shame poisons our ability to receive God's love and see ourselves the way he sees us. Shame holds us hostage to the Hiss. Such toxicity in the life of a follower of Christ! Where do we get the idea that this state is welcome for a woman of God? For one who has been *redeemed* by Jesus?

Paul wrote in 2 Corinthians 7:10: "Godly sorrow brings repentance that leads to salvation and leaves no regret." Let's take these phrases one at a time and follow the progression accomplished when we bring our guilt to Jesus.

1. Godly sorrow brings repentance. When I mess up, in *real* error, I am sorry and want to repent—to turn in the opposite way of my offense and try again. *I'm sorry! I messed up! Please forgive me!*

2. Repentance leads to salvation. When I see my failure for what it is, and turn away from it and toward the help I have in Christ, I am saved from my sin and freed to live differently. *My sorrow gives me access to Jesus' act on the cross for me. He died for me—to save me from my sins.*

3. Salvation leaves no regret. Rather than haunt us in our

middle-of-the-night dreams or accuse us in our inner beings, salvation *frees* us from needing do-overs. *Jesus' death on the cross for me, and my embrace of his offering for my sin, results in freedom for me. I don't look back. I move ahead. I'm dead to sin and alive to Christ.*

Good stuff for the one who is connected to such power in Jesus.

Then comes the second part of verse 10: "Godly sorrow brings repentance that leads to salvation and leaves no regret, *but worldly sorrow brings death*" (emphasis added).

Unlike the "godly sorrow" that prods us to confess our need for (and receive) help from Jesus, worldly sorrow—which is shame—*kills*. Us. Relationships. Hopes and dreams. Potential.

Slowly, like a cat sucking the breath out of a baby mouse.

Quickly and cleanly, like a wolf snapping the neck of its prey.

Perpetually, offering a poison that creates in us a thirst for yet another sip of its toxicity.

And often *secretly*, whispering to us, "You are the only one . . . No one else suffers with such inadequacy . . . Everyone else is truly qualified . . . You are the only one who is so dirty . . . so unwanted . . . so completely lacking."

In their book, *The Cure*, John Lynch, Bruce McNicol, and Bill Thrall wrote,

This shame—this self-awareness of their "uncleanness"— prompted Adam and Eve to fashion masks from leaves to hide what they now feared was true about them. It wasn't just that they'd done something wrong. They were both convinced something was now uniquely and terribly wrong about them, with them. This is how shame works, and it's different from guilt. Guilt wants to lead us to forgiveness, to be cleaned. Shame drives us to hide, convinced we cannot truly be for-given or made clean.[3]

As I enter the decade called 6-0, I'm stunned that I still struggle with shame—such powerful feelings that I'm not enough or that I'm too much. Even with all I've been invited into, all I've accomplished, all I've discovered, I still feel inadequate and incompetent in too many moments and, therefore, so wrong.

Why do I struggle so? God loves me! He really, truly loves *me*! And you! He sees us the way he made us: *beautiful*. "See what great love the Father has lavished on us, that we should be called children of God!" (1 John 3:1).

Little Elisa still crouches in the corners of my being. My eyes scan her presence again. The dirt, the grime, the mess . . . Slowly I wonder at what I'm seeing. She's not just Little Elisa. I've made her *Bad* Elisa. Her neediness is my not-enoughness. Her unmet longing is my irritatingly insatiable hunger. Her inability to right her world is my failure to fix mine.

I've been unfair to her. It's not her fault that my father aban-doned our family when she was five. She's not to blame for my mother's overdrinking. She is not "too much," as she fears. She didn't make an unfixable mess by her neediness. On the con-trary, as with all children, she simply *was*: a child with questions and needs and, most of all, a desire to be loved no matter what.

She still is a child with questions and needs. And she still does want to be loved no matter what.

And she's not bad. Shame veils the reality of her giftedness from my appreciation.

I look again. There are resilient patches of golden hope threaded in her being. She has survived. A giggle lies just behind the fear in her eyes, eager for an invitation to escape. Her bright wit and visionary view of life yearns for engagement.

God loves her. He sees her as full of beauty.

I need to learn to love Bad Elisa—the needy, sinful, messed-up me—the way God loves her. Just as God sees her through the sacrifice of his Son—restored, redeemed, beautiful—I need to see her as restored, redeemed, beautiful. Without shame.

Shameless.

Shame free.

Unashamed.

I also need to learn to love the Good Elisa—the giving and loyal, funny and resilient, dedicated and diligent—the way God loves her. Just as God sees her through the sacrifice of his Son— restored, redeemed, beautiful—I need to see her as restored, redeemed, beautiful. Without shame.

Shameless.

Shame free.

Unashamed.

I need to see *all* of me the way God sees *all* of me: through the sacrifice of his Son.

As my pastor, Robert Gelinas, puts it, "When we know God,

we have the mind of Christ. So use it! Learn to see yourself from his perspective!"

Jesus came to cancel the shamefest. Squeezing his godly essence into the body of a baby, born in a dirty manger to regular human folks, walking the dusty paths and touching the unclean with his divinity, bending under the disrespect of religious leaders, and finally enduring the humiliating scourge of sin for our sakes, Jesus *died* and then conquered death in order that shame itself might be killed. So that shame can kill us no more.

I turn and consider Little Elisa's presence, and it hits me. Jesus loves the little children. He challenged his followers to bring them to him: "Let the little children come to me, and do not hinder them" (Luke 18:16).

Jesus loves Little Elisa and Big Elisa, Bad Elisa and Good Elisa. As a redeemed follower of Christ, can I follow Jesus' work and love her as well?

At the turn of the first millennium, a monk named Bernard of Clairvaux clarified four stages of love, each building in maturity on the others:

1. Love of self for self's sake.
2. Love of God for self's sake.
3. Love of God for God's sake.
4. Love of self for God's sake.[4]

A millennium later, Rueben P. Job wrote in his book *Three Simple Questions: Knowing the God of Love, Hope, and Purpose,* "God loves us as though each one of us was the only child of

God in the world, just as God loves every other human being on the face of the earth."[5] My grandson was an "only child" and an "only grandchild" for a decade. I know firsthand how much love he has been loved with. Stunning. Early believers and modern-day saints both seem to have understood well what I'm still stumbling through. I understand it for my grandchild. Why is it so hard to own for myself?

Jesus sees Little Elisa with her bruises and messiness and loves her so. Jesus sees Big Elisa and is pleased with her strivings to know and grow in who he has made her to be. Jesus sees Bad Elisa and has freed her from her failings, real or imagined. Jesus sees Good Elisa and smiles at her efforts and yet releases her from the ongoing strain. Jesus loves *all* of Elisa, *so very much.* Can I? Can I take yet another baby step to love God back and bring myself to Jesus?

Mandy Arioto nailed it when she wrote, "We women are hard on ourselves. We have been taught to look at ourselves as an assemblage of trouble spots, a miasma of flaws. But it is time to call a truce. To learn how to like ourselves—to treat ourselves like we'd treat a best friend."[6]

Down I go in a crouch, my lap open, my eyes smiling, my arms wide to welcome. She hesitates, wondering at my sincerity. I nod and wait while she shyly approaches, one shuffling step at a time, until—at last—she climbs aboard, wraps her arms around my neck, and tucks her face in my cheek. I return the hug and hold her until my knees slide out from under me and we rock together. Heavenly arms hold us both. Little and big. Bad and good. Shamed and, more importantly, redeemed. Together at last.

Becoming Beauty Full You

1. Little/Big . . . Bad/Good

Shame keeps us from loving ourselves the way God loves us. Shame then keeps us from seeing ourselves the way God sees us. How have you separated out the parts of you into "Little" and "Big," "Bad" and "Good"? How do you need to see each part the way God sees you—through his Son's sacrifice? What would it mean for you to bring *all* of yourself to Jesus?

2. 2 Corinthians 7:10

Memorize this verse: "Godly sorrow brings repentance that leads to salvation and leaves no regret, but worldly sorrow brings death."

Use it to test the Hiss that continues in your days. If you need to repent, do so. If you have, move into "no regret."

3. Four Stages of Love

Review Bernard of Clairvaux's four stages of love. Identify which stage characterizes your current understanding of love. How is God nudging you onward?

1. Love of self for self's sake.
2. Love of God for self's sake.
3. Love of God for God's sake.
4. Love of self for God's sake.

four

LIVING LOVED

There is nothing more beautiful than a woman
who knows she is loved.

—Heidi McLaughlin[1]

My mother, Paige, died when I was thirty-five years old. Way too early for me to have been finished processing all her investments in me, the good and the not-so-good.

At the time, I was almost grateful she was gone. I know, that sounds horrific for me to admit. But in the thick work of moving away from who I thought she needed and wanted me to be and toward who I sensed God calling me to become, my energy was focused on creating necessary boundaries. And in that season of identity formation, I pushed heavily against Paige rather than pulling for Elisa. Such is often the work of young adulthood.

After my parents divorced, I effortlessly slipped into the role of Hero in the ACOA (Adult Child of An Alcoholic) constellation, in which every family member takes on a preferred role as a means of coping with the disease.[2] I took care of my younger brother, made sure my mother was up and off to work in the morning, cleaned our house, and made most of the meals. (Admittedly, my cooking skills were limited, but at least we ate.) I'm not trying to sound heroic, because I actually wasn't heroic. I was just surviving, and this is the role that fit my personality: take charge and do what's needed—and deny that you have any needs yourself. Be the good one. Codepend: create worth for yourself by intuiting and then meeting the needs of everyone else around you, so that you are dependent on them being dependent on you, and you are in control—or at least more in control.

My brother and sister chose roles that suited them as well. Kirby's was the Scapegoat, the one sometimes in trouble and sure to distract from the problems of the alcoholic. He pushed against Mother, too, and forayed into this and that issue, but he also leaned into her dramatic side, embracing what he always described as her "Auntie Mame" quirkiness. As he matured into his midtwenties, he and Mother grew close.

Cathy had chosen the Lost Child role, shedding our family as soon as her independence allowed. She left Houston—and us—for college and never returned. A silent, stiff-armed rebuff wedged between her and Mother. *Don't come near me.*

Of course, none of us knew such elements were at work until much later in life. I was just starting to discover my role preference and codependence when my mother was diagnosed with cancer and began a rapid decline, closing in on death just six months later.

I flew to her bedside, where we three children arrived one at a time to sit vigil for several days. Kirby, closest to her Fort Worth, Texas, home, drove up from Houston and arrived first.

He had called to hurry me down from Denver. Cathy was on her way but wouldn't arrive until the next morning.

On the plane on my way down, I stared out the window, rehearsing my recently learned need for boundaries and my mother's historic need for help. While compassion and grief nosed about the periphery of my thoughts, like two strays looking for a place to curl up and rest, my resident-guard-dog senses were on high alert. Just that past summer, when she had come up for a visit, my mother had laid out her hopes that I would feed her and take care of her. While I knew she was sick, my insides tightened and my heart hurt. Hadn't I fed her and taken care of her my whole life?

No. I didn't want to go there again, back to such necessary-ness for her that I lost myself. I couldn't.

I walked into Mother's hospital room, defended. The fluorescent light above her bed had been switched to ambient mode, casting both soft shadows and hushed highlights. At her bedside, Kirby looked up in relief. He filled me in on her status and told me that when he had arrived, she had cried and told him over and over that she loved him and how much it meant to her to have him there. He was so glad he had been able to get there speedily.

Shrunken in her illness, my mother opened her eyes and weakly smiled at me. I hugged her and sat atop the egg-crate mattress, holding her hand. I told her I loved her and was so sorry she was in pain. She smiled again and thanked me. Then she asked when my sister would arrive, and she dozed off.

Kirby and I were still there when Cathy came through the curtained doorway early the next morning. Immediately

Mother reached out her arms toward my sister. As Cathy awkwardly endured her embrace, Mother cried and told Cathy how much she loved her. They were words Kirby and I had expected. Mother had yearned for her oldest daughter's return, the "setting right" of a broken relationship. We often work hardest for the love of the one who most strongly withholds it.

Over the next few days, we three took turns spelling each other in our deathwatch. When Mother did pass, Cathy was with her, holding her hand. It seemed right.

In the decades since my mother's death, I've uncovered layer after layer of her needs, my needs, and our needs. Her failures and my triumphs. Her investments and my infractions. Her neediness and my not-neediness. Our sibling arrivals at her deathbed scene have haunted me. Something about each reunion hung on me. Mother had so ardently received Kirby and told him of her love. She'd practically panted to receive Cathy, and even in the depletion of her life she had found words to profess her love to her eldest child, over and over.

With me she had smiled and received my embrace. I'm the one who said, "I love you." Not her.

It riddled me.

When I brought it up to Kirby, he downplayed my memory. Yes, he had seen the hungry exchange she had with Cathy, but he chalked that up to Mother's need to bring her lost daughter home. I had always been there. To him, Mother loved me *best*. Better than either Cathy or himself. Kirby continued: Mother knew I would always be there. She didn't need to tell me she loved me. She knew I knew.

But did I? Did I *really* know my mother loved me? On some level, sure, I knew. My mother was never intentionally mean to me. She creatively planned themed birthday parties, relinquished her resolve never to have a cat to my unceasing pleading for a little black kitten, and one Christmas replaced the paintings above the couch with beautifully hung clothes—department-window style—all for me. She called me every single Sunday afternoon of my adult life. She was understandably terrified when I met and married Evan, because he had survived cancer and we knew we would be unable to have children biologically. But then she got to know Evan and fully embraced him and each of our children as we adopted them. She was thrilled when I stepped into radio land with my own program. She had been a pioneer as a woman in radio way back in the day, and she took joy in her reproductive reality when I entered that world. We shared body types and coloring and a creative flair. In many ways, when my mother looked at me, she saw herself. And it was good.

All this shininess was dulled by an addiction that tarnished love into what was not love. By the casting of her human needs on me to meet for her. By the leakage of her responsibilities into buckets with my name on them to pick up and carry for her.

When I sorted out the good and not-so-good, the good came out ahead. Yes, I knew my mother loved me. But I needed to hear it. Why did she have to withhold what I needed? Why did it always have to be about her and her illness? She was the parent; I was the child! She died without saying to me what she had said to her other two children: "I love you."

Recently—just a few months ago—I figured something out.

I was out riding my bike down the trails behind my house, the ones facing the Rockies. The thought came, bright and clear and unmistakable: *Elisa, she didn't tell you that she loved you because you wouldn't let her.*

Oh my.

It was true. My necessary barriers—vital for my self-release from my codependent Hero role—had become an impenetrable armor. My mother was smart and respectful, and she was likely spent enough to know she wasn't going to get through my defenses. So she played her assigned part in our relationship. It's not just the "well" ones who follow such roles in family systems. She leaned back and received the love I commanded her to receive, in the way I directed her to receive it. And I missed out on the love she wanted to offer me.

I wonder if I ever do such a thing with others. With my husband? With my children? With my friends? Do I not let them love me? And if I don't, why is that?

Do I do that with God?

God loves me. How do I move beyond the Hiss and shed the shame that keeps me hostage, so that I can truly see myself the way God sees me? By letting him love me. Because only when we let God love us can we see ourselves the way he sees us: beautiful.

Henri Nouwen was a priest who similarly struggled to grasp God's love for him. In his book *The Return of the Prodigal Son*, Nouwen traces his discovery of Rembrandt's painting of that title and the hours he spent sitting before it in its home museum, The Hermitage, in Saint Petersburg, Russia. Having been given special permission through a series of networked relationships and events, Nouwen spent a total of four focused hours in front of the huge painting, examining the perspective of each character illustrated both in the painting and in the parable told by Jesus in Luke 15: the anguished father, the remote elder son, and the prodigal. Nouwen learned to see himself in each portrayal.

Near the end of his book, Nouwen made a climactic discovery, an understanding opened to him much like the secret wardrobe door revealed a new world in C. S. Lewis's *The Lion, the Witch and the Wardrobe*. He had assumed all his life that he was to orient himself, in the posture of a sincerely seeking pilgrim, toward finding God. But through the view of the seeking father, Nouwen grasped that he was to let himself be found by this hunting Sovereign. This recognition—that God was looking for him, seeking him, moving toward him, loving him—changed Nouwen's life.

In stunned wonder, Nouwen discovered,

> The question is not "How am I to find God?" but "How am I to let myself be found by him?" The question is not "How am I to know God?" but "How am I to let myself be known by God?" And, finally, the question is not "How am I to love God?" but "How am I to let myself be loved by God?"[3]

Reeling under these realizations, Henri's perception of God was forever changed by how he understood that God sees him. Absorbing God from Rembrandt's multidimensional artist's perspective, he marveled,

I am beginning now to see how radically the character of my spiritual journey will change when I no longer think of God as hiding out and making it as difficult as possible for me to find him, but, instead, as the one who is looking for me while I am doing the hiding.[4]

As Nouwen asked, "Wouldn't it be wonderful to make God smile by giving God the chance to find me and love me lavishly?"[5]

I hesitate. It sounds so appealing. I'm drawn forward, toward this golden hope. And then I stop.

Love me lavishly? *Me?*

I struggle.

A friend of mine opened up a passage of Scripture and showed me something I hadn't seen before. She showed me the description of Jesus' baptism. Here's what Matthew wrote:

As soon as Jesus was baptized, he went up out of the water. At that moment heaven was opened, and he saw the Spirit of God descending like a dove and alighting on him. And a voice from heaven said, "This is my Son, whom I love; with him I am well pleased." (Matthew 3:16–17)

With you I am well pleased.

Okay, God, through the Holy Spirit, is talking about Jesus— perfect Jesus. Of course he is well pleased with Jesus.

But my friend dug deeper: "If God is well pleased with Jesus—and he sees us *through* Jesus and his act on the cross for us, in which we trust—then maybe—just maybe—God is well pleased with us too?"

Later, on my own, I pulled up my trusty Logos Bible Software and did a little word study on the term *well pleased.* Heady truths cataloged in columns across my computer screen. To summarize, the voice from heaven is God the Father, and he's puffed-chest proud of his Son—his *favorite* and *chosen* and *approved* and yes, *perfect* Son.[6] In this term, *well pleased,* God offers an endorsement of Jesus as his Son, both for who he is and for what he will do for humankind: redeem us and return us to God's original intent for us. Humankind includes *me.*

So, because of Jesus, could God be well pleased with me? Enough to love me? All of me? And lavishly?

Frightening!

Several years ago I stood in church, mouthing the projected words of a worship song. While I was present in the moment, my mind wandered.

Suddenly an arm reached around my shoulder and a mouth bent to my ear. "God has a promise for you that you have not believed him for. If you believe him, he will fulfill it and overcome the past."

I looked up. Pastor Richard lifted his head from my ear, met my gaze, gave me a sideways hug, and walked away. The singing continued, but it was his words that vibrated in my ears. I had no idea what he was talking about.

Now, please understand that our church is a body of believers from all kinds of denominations—Baptist, Methodist, Catholic,

Presbyterian. Diversity in denomination is matched by diversity in race, in age, in political views, in what's "wrong" with us (addiction, financial need, pride, and so on), and in expression of our worship. That Pastor Richard spoke such a statement in my ear was surprising but not unheard of. I just couldn't figure out what the utterance he shared meant for me.

I wrote the words on a sticky note and put it on my computer monitor for a season. Now and then I would pause and consider their possible meaning, with no additional revelation. A few months later at a church gathering, I asked Pastor Richard what he thought they meant. He said he didn't know. Eventually I moved the sticky note to the inside cover of my current journal, where I would reflect now and then on the meaning.

Like I said, that was several years ago. I have to admit that I never did understand those two sentences.

Until now. Literally—in these moments writing this book.

"God has a promise for you that you have not believed him for. If you believe him, he will fulfill it and overcome the past."

God loves me. Will I let him?

I think about all the ways I don't let myself be loved. With a friend, I'd rather be on the giving end than the owing end, you know? With my husband, mercy, for sure I let him love me. But to be honest, I'm most comfy letting him love me in ways where I maintain a bit of control. Intimacy can be so *vulnerable*. With my kids, I'm not sure. They're still doing that approach/avoid stuff they need to do in order to be adult children and, maybe one day, adults period.

With God? Can I let him love me? All of me? Is that safe?

Can I embrace what Philip Yancey suggests? "Not the least of Jesus' accomplishments is that he made us somehow lovable to God."[7]

I'd like to. But there's something else pushing back. It's deeper than the "I'm a toad" objection. I know we are all toads at times. I know that I know that I know that Jesus died on the cross as a payment for my toadiness—for all of our croaky uglinesses. I know he loves me in spite of me.

So I walk around myself, taking stock again. Like a tourist taking in a sculpture in an Italian museum, I look up and down, from the back and the front. I peer into the irisless eyes, down into the inner parts of me. Like Michelangelo, I back myself into the mind of God and take a meandering stroll through his eyes' gallery of just how he imagines each of his prodigal beings. And I see. Just a teensy bit, but enough to pull the realization forward:

I am *loved*. By God.

My steps stutter. Even if God is safer than any human, able to love me for me and not for his need meeting, an *aha!* emerges. I'm afraid. I wasn't loved well by those who were supposed to love me well, and as a result I'm afraid to let myself be loved by the perfect Lover. The Author of love. The Artist who paints me into the canvas of his world, who sees who I already am in him, dipping his brush into crimson oil to sign his creation before I'm fully finished. The One who invites me to step around to his side of the easel to view me the way he does.

In response to the Facebook survey I posted, one woman wrote,

I felt from childhood that I could only be loved if I did everything right. So I thought I was doomed. I found myself at a church service where the pastor stopped midsentence and said, "I feel I need to say this: there is someone here who needs to know that God LOVES them, and if they don't understand this, they won't understand the rest of it."[8]

Her pastor's words resonate with me now. I need to know, to believe, that God loves me, and if I don't understand this, I can't understand the rest of it.

I remember back to Pastor Richard's whispered words over me: *"God has a promise for you that you have not believed him for. If you believe him, he will fulfill it and overcome the past."*

Help me, God, to let you love me.

Suddenly I'm the cripple by the pool at Bethesda in John 5, the one who had been an invalid for thirty-eight years when Jesus came and asked, "Do you want to get well?" (John 5:6).

Do I?

My heart aches at what seems at first to be my surprising, though unintentional, betrayal of God. What if *Jesus* didn't let God the Father love him? What if he had pulled back from the dove embrace, pooh-poohed the heavenly endorsement? I realize this learning to let God love me is going to take effort and large doses of risk. Maybe it comes naturally to some, like children. But to those of us who've been disappointed or wounded, learning to be loved—letting God love us—is a life's work. An intentional daily exercise in which we first inspect, then identify, and slowly release unnecessary defenses against the very One who already sees and still loves.

Writing about the living Word—Jesus—the author of the book of Hebrews said,

> For the word of God is alive and active. Sharper than any double-edged sword, it penetrates even to dividing soul and spirit, joints and marrow; it judges the thoughts and attitudes of the heart. Nothing in all creation is hidden from God's sight. Everything is uncovered and laid bare before the eyes of him to whom we must give account. (Hebrews 4:12–13)

Such a see-through-me kind of love isn't the awful reality we might assume. Rather, because Jesus sees us through himself, he loves us completely. Really. Just as we are. In his gaze, we are secure and safe.

My mother and father had difficulty loving me. I have difficulty being loved. I want to get well. I want to be different. I want to be loved and to love. I want to see how God sees me. And I realize I can't see how God sees me—much less accept his pronouncement that I'm beautiful—until I let him love me.

I step forward. I lower my shield. I lift my face. I receive God's pronouncement over me: *"This is my beloved. In her I am well pleased."* I let him love me.

God loves me. I love him back by letting him. And when I let God love me, and only then, I can see myself the way he sees me.

Becoming Beauty Full You

1. The Return of the Prodigal Son

Go online and take a deep, searching look at Rembrandt's painting that so affected Henri Nouwen. Imagine yourself in the role of each character. Then imagine how God loves you in each role.

2. Quit

What is your "work" in learning to let God love you? Fill in the blank for yourself:

Quit trying to be _____ , *and learn to let God love you.*

3. Well Pleased

Reread God's words over Jesus, and insert your own name in the sentence: *This is my beloved,* _____ . *In* _____ *I am well pleased.* Imagine God seeing *you* through Jesus.

part two

BEAUTY

Seeing Your Beauty the Way God Does

In 1756 philosopher Edmund Burke wrote, "We must conclude that beauty is, for the greater part, some quality in bodies acting mechanically upon the human mind by the intervention of the senses."[1] Supposedly, his words form one of the most applauded definitions of beauty ever. Huh?

Beauty is a tricky trait. And please note, I'm not trying to present a full-scale examination of a topic experts in every category have debated for *centuries*. I'm also not talking about *pretty, hot, cute, cool, attractive* here. Yet, as we dive into how God sees us as *beauty* full, it's surely helpful to provide a definition of how I'm using the term.

First, some background.

In the brain's medial frontal cortex, certain patterns of activity are associated with viewing something beautiful.[2] So there's that: a *physical* reaction to beauty.

In his acclaimed *Six Names of Beauty*, Crispin Sartwell attributed beauty neither to the subject nor to the object, but to the relation between them, and even more widely also to the context where they connect.[3] Thus, beauty involves how we interact with our world. There's an *emotional* element.

In the thirteenth century, Thomas Aquinas identified three requirements of beauty: integrity (or perfection), consonance, and clarity.[4] Beauty holds a certain component of balance, which provides *cognitive* pleasure.

Different cultures interpret beauty in various ways, evidenced by the multiple definitions of their words for beauty in their own languages. In Navajo, *hozho* is "health, harmony." Sanskrit uses *sundara* to express "whole, holy." English's *beauty* means "the object of longing."[5]

The two main original languages in the Bible treat beauty distinctly as well. In Hebrew, the word *yapha* means "glow, bloom." This is the word used to describe Sarah, Abraham's wife, as beautiful, and the same word has the sense of *right* or *appropriate* in Ecclesiastes 3:11: "He has made everything beautiful in its time."[6] Several Greek words for beauty are seen in the New Testament. One is *kalos*, meaning "ideal or good," the word Jesus used of Mary's act when she anointed his body in Mark 14:6: "She has done a beautiful thing to me."

Physical. Emotional. Cognitive. Health, harmony, whole, holy, longing. Glow, bloom, right, ideal, good. All concepts that are helpful when approaching the topic of beauty.

But to me, and for our purposes, perhaps David Hume's comment from 1757 makes the most sense: "Beauty is no quality in things themselves: it exists merely in the mind which contemplates them; and each mind perceives a different beauty."[7] To put this phrase in current, familiar terms, "Beauty is in the eye of the beholder."

And our "beholder" is God.

Beauty is how God sees us, through Jesus. And as such, beauty emerges as our identity in Christ.

In part 2 we'll look at beauty from this perspective: how God sees us. We'll discover five places in which God sees us (and therefore, we can see ourselves) as beautiful: *voice, vessel, womb, scar,* and *sway.* Some of these characteristics will be slam dunks for you, elementary elements you mastered long ago on your journey with Jesus. In such chapters, focus your attention on brushing up, remembering, and growing further through the strength you find there.

Other aspects will be more challenging. They're like potholes you've driven around most of your days. Stuck points you prefer to avoid. Black-bottomed puddles you don't even want to go near. Nevertheless, such elements express more of the "you" God made—beauty full you.

Hello! God loves us. We love him back by letting him love us. When we let God love us—and *only* then—are we at last able to see ourselves as he does: as beauty-filled beings.

five

VOICE

Beauty in Your Unique Personality

She was beautiful, but not like those girls in the magazines. She was beautiful, for the way she thought. She was beautiful, for that sparkle in her eyes when she talked about something she loved. She was beautiful, for her ability to make other people smile even if she was sad. No, she wasn't beautiful for something as temporary as her looks. She was beautiful, deep down to her soul.

—Source unknown

As a toddler, my first word was not a word. My mother's version of the story is that I was a late talker. No "Mama," "Dada," "Kitty," "Doggie" for me. Mother was so worried that she took me to a special doctor's appointment when I was well over a year old—maybe eighteen months. The doctor examined me, listened to my babbling coos, and sent me home, telling my perplexed mother that I would talk when I was ready.

A few weeks later, as Mother lifted my pudgy body into my high chair for lunch, I stiffened my legs and refused. She speared me back down between the tray and chair, and again I balked. After yet another try and my refusal, my mother lowered me to the linoleum tile floor and stared down at the stubborn frown above my bib and the tears welling up in my eyes. What now?

"I don't want that chair! I want this one!" I announced, pointing away from the high chair and toward the regular-size chair at the table next to me.

I'd found my voice.

But then I lost it again.

Seasons of uncertainty from my parents' divorce and my mother's struggle with alcohol shushed my voice silent. My conflicted pubescence, which bloomed into young womanhood in a world where a woman's place was anything but "known," resulted in a stuttering expression of "me." At times I boldly paraded at the head of the pack. In other moments I rehearsed other people's lines, mimicking someone else's way of being as my own. There were moments when I was flat-out ordered to shut up. Children should be seen and not heard. Women don't have a vote. You have to earn the right to be heard. As a result, I shamed my voice mute.

We all do this—find and lose our voices. Voice is the expression of our unique personalities or identities. Such a core first element of beauty! We learn to speak our minds. Then we learn to hold our tongues.

We women vary when it comes to being comfortable knowing—and using—our voices. For some, voice is a clear element of identity and selfhood. Convinced of who we are and what we have to offer, we open our mouths with a trill of contribution. Others find voice confusing: What to say? When to say it? We "But...but...but..." our way through interactions, unsure of whether we're even making a contribution. From lack of use, some voices have simply gone missing in tongue-tied atrophy. Then there are voices that have been duct-taped still, turned into a low-pitched hum of terror deep in the throat that dares not emerge.

Girl Talk

Whoever we are as women, most of us still struggle with voice in some ages and areas, seasons and settings. What is it about "girl talk" that can be so not encouraged? Perhaps we've bought into the "too" messages around us.

Women use too many words.

Stereotypes abound accusing women of talking *way* more than men. You may have heard that on average women use twenty thousand words each day, compared to a man's seven thousand. That's thirteen *thousand* more words! Such a statistic can make you lick your lips and shut them quick. But in her research, linguistics scholar and author of *You Just Don't Understand* Deborah Tannen discovered such an assumption is bunk. Citing follow-up studies and broader research, Tannen emphasizes that men and women use about the same number of words each day—more like sixteen thousand each—and the number of words in a day depends on the situation and what the words are being used for. Men tend to use "report-talk," where they offer stories and information, while women use "rapport-talk," which focuses on personal relationships and experiences. She concludes it's not that women talk *more* than men; it's that women and men talk *differently*.[1]

There are many days I fall far short of sixteen thousand words. Sure, I love to debrief life with my husband, and I do so just about every chance I get. But Evan commutes to another state biweekly for work, and while we're faithful to catching up on the phone, there's no way our daily efforts tally up more than three or four thousand words. And can I just say he loves to talk with me too? I spend plenty of time happily listening.

Women use too many words with too many emotions.

Because Eve took the first bite of the fruit, women have been labeled as the weaker sex. Duped by the serpent into eating forbidden fruit, the woman is seen as gullible, acting with her heart and not her head. (Interesting. As I think it over, weakness could exist in being the first to sin—but also in being the second, couldn't it?)

Football legend John Elway's voice caught in his throat as he announced his retirement from the NFL. Intrigued by this strong man's soft heart, we leaned in with compassion and knowingness. Ten years later, he broke into tears again as he press-conferenced the retirement of the owner of the Denver

Broncos as a result of the onset of Alzheimer's disease, a man who was a father-figure to Elway. We don't think of Elway as *weak* for leaking out his emotions. Nothing but! We *warm* to him. But when several US women's hockey team members cried after their loss to Canada in the 2014 Olympic games, mocking jeers sounded![2]

It's not just the emotion of sadness that labels women "too." What about anger? Men can raise their voices, confront with force, wave their arms with emphasis, even pound the table—and be seen as strong and leader-worthy. Women? Any such gesture categorizes the user as a witch with a *B*. I've experienced this firsthand. Once a staff member referred to my emphatic insistence on meeting a financial goal as being "over the top."

Women use too many words with too many
emotions in too many settings.

Women are told to speak up for the poor but to be quiet regarding the Bible, to run schools and hospitals and other services that educate and heal but to stay out of executive leadership. For as long as we've been on the planet, women have been scuttled off to the margins to stifle their voices and removed from the masses where their influence can be heard and felt.

I remember being asked to "share" in chapel at a Bible college where I taught early in my career. This was the specific word used in the invitation: *share*. I wasn't to preach, but rather to share. I wondered just what that meant. Was I to share from my own life rather than from the Bible? How was *that* helpful to anyone? Confused, I put together a talk that illustrated how God was weaving lessons into my every day, with the focus on God and not on me. It worked. Students were encouraged. But the experience left me wobbly in my voice. Sharing was acceptable. Preaching—or just using the Bible to make my points in mixed company—was "too."

Which "too" silences your voice? What ones duct-tape your mouth shut? Too young? Too old? Too smart? Too uneducated? Too weak? Too powerful? Too outgoing? Too shy? Too sexy? Too prudish? Too feminine? Too masculine? Too assertive? Too submissive? Mercy! The Hiss is still at work!

How healthy is your voice? How convinced are you of the uniqueness and significance of your identity and personhood in your world? *Hello!* God loves you, dear *beauty.* He sees—hears!—your voice as *beauty full.*

Spiritual Voice: A Symphony in Three Notes

When we see our voices as God does, we can know our voices in truth. Who are *you*? What makes you a person with identity? The funny thing is that what makes us unique and significant as individuals in our world actually begins with how God made us *alike* as women. The work of Carolyn Custis James has deeply influenced how I understand God's creative process in forming all of us as women—and how our value and purpose as women are intertwined with the value and purpose of men. She suggested we women were made for three consistent purposes:

1. We are image bearers. Together with men, women express the image of God in our world. Both genders are essential to representing who God is. "So God created mankind in his own image, in the image of God he created them; male and female he created them" (Genesis 1:27).

2. We are *ezers*. The Hebrew word, translated as "strong helper," is used twenty-one times in the Old Testament. In sixteen occurrences, *ezer* is used of God, as Israel's strong helper. While sometimes translated in Genesis 2:18 as "help meet," a more consistent rendering would be to call a woman a "strong helper" here as well: "It is not good for the man to be alone. I will make a helper suitable for him" (Genesis 2:18).

3. We are colaborers. Together with men, women are necessary to carrying out God's purposes in our world. Both genders, forming a "blessed alliance," are required to complete God's work. "God blessed them and said to them, 'Be fruitful and increase in number; fill the earth and subdue it'" (Genesis 1:28).[3]

As Lisa Bevere put it, "Paradise had a problem and we [women] were God's answer."[4] Woot!

I muse over how God has created and called forth *me* as a woman for his purposes. How empowering to see my voice as God sees it! I view God's image in my being. I lift the weapon of my femaleness in defense of all that is righteous. I link arms with my brothers to work God's good pleasure in our world. I see my spiritual voice as God sees it, and it is magnificent!

Can you see this? *Your* voice is the ongoing essence of who God made you to be: a spiritual being who is an image bearer, an *ezer,* and a colaborer in God's world with men. That's powerful! But wait—there's more: God creates *every* woman with this three-note symphony of voice. Your sister. Your mom. Your daughter. Your girlfriend.

We women, *all* of us and *every* one of us, share a gendered calling to live out our influence on this planet for God's ultimate purposes. Embracing our alikeness in voice as women is the beginning of seeing ourselves the way God sees us.

God also shaped each of us with an individual voice, gifting us to offer a unique and significant contribution in our world. He has placed in you a voice that no one else can duplicate. Ever.

Personal Voice: Timbre!

Just as the whorls of a fingerprint are unique to each human digit, so are the timbres of voice. No two human voices are alike. The size and shape of our vocal chords, along with the size and shape of the rest of our bodies, together offer a sound that is wholly and completely unique to the person uttering it.[5] Soprano, alto, tenor, bass, and all the derivations in between.

Similarly, personality is unique to every person. In addition to containing our spiritual beings, our voices express the ever-developing essences of our personal beings: our personalities and identities.

For centuries, experts have identified "types" and "categories." Such slots help us to better understand ourselves and each other.

- What animal are you? Lion, otter, beaver, or golden retriever?[6]
- What is your love language? Words of affirmation, quality time, receiving gifts, acts of service, or physical touch?[7]
- What is your temperament? Sanguine, choleric, melancholic, or phlegmatic?[8]
- What is your Type? E (Extrovert) or I (Introvert), S (Sensing) or N (Intuitive), T (Thinking) or F (Feeling), J (Judging) or P (Perceiving)?[9]
- What is your role preference at work? Dominance, influence, steadiness, or conscientiousness?[10]
- What's your number on the Enneagram?[11]
- What spiritual gifts do you possess?[12]

At times we resist such categorization, because any typing at all seems to fight our uniqueness as persons with personalities. How can a column, an animal, or a set of letters contain the essence of *me*? How can I fit the same label my mom fits and yet still be unique?

Labels can't define us, but they can help us identify some of the elements that make us "us" and then nudge us forward to grow into all we can uniquely be. Whoever *you* are . . . you *are*. And *you* uniquely invest the significance of your spiritual and personal being through your voice.

So how do we recognize our own God-formed, unique voices?

Voice Recognition

The process of recognizing, defining, owning, and investing my voice has been hard all along for me. I shouldn't be surprised, since it took me nearly two years to mouth a sentence. Sixty years later, I'm still wrapping my tongue around the essence of Elisa.

For decades—five, maybe?—much of me was revealed through whatever I was *doing* at the time. My voice was expressed in and through the roles I occupied. As a child I was dramatic and wooing. My mother's favorite nickname for me was "Sarah Bernhardt"—the silent film star—likely a vestige of my slowness to speak. In junior high my voice copycatted trends of popularity. In adolescence I yo-yoed between fears of being too much or not enough. When I was single, I was flirtatious and bubbly. As a young seminary student, I was still bubbly but also earnestly focused. The newly married me nested and bonded and grew while also wrestling with my individual voice since becoming permanently linked to another person. The Dean of Women Elisa carved out a vulnerable leadership alongside students not so very much younger. Mother Elisa was nervous and nurturing and swoopingly present. CEO me became ardent and visional in honest realness and transformational effectiveness.

Today, after stepping down from full-time leadership and into a solo ministry of speaking and writing, a "less necessary" Elisa brings me full circle back to just being me. A me with no staff to lead and a much-reduced personal world, since by now my kids are pretty much gone. Just who the rest of this me is, I'm still discovering!

Jane Stephens and Stephen Zades, experts in their field of personal identity, defined voice as more than just what we do or the various roles we occupy in life: "[Voice] begins with one's ability to own oneself, and it grows with one's ability to give that self to the world. . . . Voice is an artesian well, the best resource in each person."[13] I love that! Don't you? Such a positive and powerful calling forth of who we are and how we invest ourselves in our world.

Gradually I've come to understand that roles alone don't—and never really could—*define* my voice. Rather, my voice—and yours too—*emerges* in roles, expressing chameleon-like some aspects of my being through what I am doing but never expressing *all* of Elisa at once. Today I know that my greatest offering on this planet is not in the roles I perform but in the *me* I bring to whatever moment I'm in. I'm living out the words of Richard Rohr: "All we can give back and all God wants from any of us is to humbly and proudly return the product that we have been given—which is ourselves!"[14]

I am the offering. My *voice* is what I have to invest on this planet in the people and purposes where God places me. To borrow words from Pastor Earl Creps, "My best practice must be *me*."[15]

Coming to such a stance has been challenging. Like being handed a surprising A+ test score after I hadn't studied a whit, I've pushed away this previously grandiose-seeming perspective. Isn't this *over*stating my worth, my value, my place here in this world? Isn't this just a charade to try to legitimize what isn't legitimate: me? To be honest, I struggle in writing here, tempted to run to other, more qualified voices to express the concept of voice rather than using my own. What do *I* know? I go to bed at night wrapped in insecurity and, Jacob-like, wrestle through the night. In the morning I rise, talk to God yet again, and sit down at the keyboard with him whispering, *"I love you. I made your voice for you and for my purposes. Own your voice and invest your voice in my world.* Your *voice."* I put the words on a sticky note and place it on my screen. I try to trust as I type.

Next to my keyboard my Bible lies open. "Look at the birds of the air; they do not sow or reap or store away in barns, and yet your heavenly Father feeds them. Are you not much more valuable than they?" (Matthew 6:26). I note the possessive—*your*—placed before *heavenly Father.* He's *my* heavenly Father. He is not the father of birds. He created them, sure. But he's *my* dad. And he says I'm more valuable than the birds that he takes care of. *Valuable. Worthy.* I think of a plaque I saw in a bookstore: "Your value doesn't decrease based on someone's inability to see your worth." Even if it's my own inability to see my worth.

Maybe this is it: voice is our spiritual and personal human *being* that expresses itself in our human *doing.* Our creator God formed our voices—our spiritual and personal beings—and he invites us to discover and embrace our voices and then use our voices in our doings.

During his final journey from Caesarea to Rome to defend himself on charges of heresy, the apostle Paul endured two weeks at sea in torturous weather. Hurricane-force winds drove the ship and its nearly three hundred passengers off course. All aboard—sailors, passengers, and leaders—hadn't eaten or slept in days and were in grave danger. In the deep night, an angel appeared to Paul and proclaimed that all would survive. Encouraging words, to be sure. But perhaps the most empowering strength came as Paul was reminded of the status of his *being* in relationship to God. The next morning, Paul gathered the sailors and recalled the angel's words: "Last night an angel of the God to whom I belong and whom I serve stood beside me and said, 'Do not be afraid, Paul'" (Acts 27:23–24).

The God *to whom* I belong and *whom* I serve.

The storm at sea provided an orchestration of God's faithfulness in Paul's life. He lifted his ears and listened as God played note after note for him, reminding him of just who he was on this planet. In response to God's revelation, Paul embraced his voice: his human *being* expressed in his human *doing*.

Can you and I embrace our human being (who we are) in our human doing (what we do) through our *beauty full* voices?

Falsetto Self

Once we recognize our voices, keeping them true can be tricky. Simon Tugwell wrote of our tendency to turn to a fake self rather than hold authentic:

> Like runaway slaves, we either flee our own reality or manufacture a false self which is mostly admirable, mildly prepossessing, and superficially happy. We hide what we know or feel ourselves to be (which we assume to be unacceptable

and unlovable) behind some kind of appearance which we hope will be more pleasing. We hide behind pretty faces which we put on for the benefit of our public. And in time we may even come to forget that we are hiding, and think that our assumed pretty face is what we really look like.[16]

A wise counselor—okay, my own therapist—once said that we all possess two "selves": a public self and a private self. The degree to which these two selves are the same is the measure of our authenticity. You know—you're hollering at the kids to come to the dinner table when the doorbell rings, and you open it to a Girl Scout selling cookies, and your just-a-minute-ago Cruella De Vil voice goes all Junior Asparagus-y.

Knowing your true voice helps you use it with integrity. Your true being in your authentic doing. Take me: I'll never sing a solo. I won't run for political office. I won't go into law. I probably won't do child care, other than for my own grandchildren. Instead, I clank away at a keyboard. I climb steps to a podium and fiddle with an over-the-ear mic. I plop down in neighborhood family rooms and open the Bible with others who wonder just who Jesus is today. I risk posing a question on a controversial topic in a setting when doing so might be a bit dicey, but I sense it still needs to be asked. I tease my oldest grandson with preposterous riddles. I stay in relationships with no-matter-what love.

Quaker Parker J. Palmer wrote, "Our deepest calling is to grow into our authentic selfhood, whether or not it conforms to some image of who we *ought* to be. As we do so, we will not only find the joy that every human seeks—we will also find our path of authentic service in the world."[17]

There it is again, this descriptor of voice: our being expressed in our doing.

There is something so freeing about identifying and then using voice. To *be* and then to *do;* to *do* out of our *be.* The psalmist wrote, "Hear my voice in accordance with your love" (Psalm 119:149). And I know that God does. He hears *my* voice in accordance with *his* love. And he hears *your* voice—your *beauty full* voice—in accordance with his love as well.

Several years ago while I was in Kenya with the ONE Campaign, our van of visiting Western women pulled into a village, where we were met by a colorful crowd of gorgeous women. As we emerged from our van, the group heaved with joy, clapping and smiling and yodeling out a greeting of "La la la la la!" How could we respond to their hospitality to equally convey our enthusiasm to meet them?

We lifted our voices in imitation: "La la la la la!" After my first hesitant attempt, and their twinkly-eyed gleeful reception, my throat opened, and freely and fully, I thrilled and trilled "La la la la la!" again and again until we women, who had never before met, fell into one another's arms in happy acceptance.

Your voice is your unique instrument of core identity, both spiritual and personal. God has tuned it for his pleasure and his purposes to provide significance for you and through you, for your world. Remember *whose* you are and *whom* you serve. Lift your being and your doing in your *beauty full* voice!

La la la la la!

Becoming Beauty Full You

1. Your Spiritual Voice: Listen to God

Nancy Beach summarized two specific efforts: to listen first to our lives and then to listen to God.[18] Good advice!

Start a journal to specifically consider your unique voice—both personal and spiritual—and contemplate the following questions. You might answer one question each day or take a half day to listen deeply.

- When did you first know God to be real? What was that experience like?
- How does God "speak" to you with his voice?

When Moses entered the tent of meeting to speak with the LORD, he heard the voice speaking to him from between the two cherubim above the atonement cover on the ark of the covenant law. In this way the LORD spoke to him. (Numbers 7:89)

Whether you turn to the right or to the left, your ears will hear a voice behind you saying, "This is the way; walk in it." (Isaiah 30:21)

God's voice thunders in marvelous ways;
   he does great things beyond our understanding. (Job 37:5)

And a voice from heaven said, "This is my Son, whom I love; with him I am well pleased." (Matthew 3:17)

On the last and greatest day of the festival, Jesus stood
and said in a loud voice, "Let anyone who is thirsty come
to me and drink." (John 7:37)

My sheep listen to my voice; I know them, and they follow me. (John 10:27)

I stand at the door and knock. If anyone hears my voice
and opens the door, I will come in and eat with that person, and they with me. (Revelation 3:20)

- Has God offered you a promise that he wants you to
  believe? What is it?
- What words does God use about you?
- What names does God ascribe to you?
- Which person of the Godhead do you most relate
  to: God the Father, God the Son, or God the Holy
  Spirit? Why do you think this is the case? How can
  you get to know the other persons in the Trinity?
- Review the three elements of female identity
  suggested by Carolyn Custis James and consider
  how you do or don't embrace each: image bearer,
  ezer (strong helper), colaborer with men.
- What are your spiritual gifts? Are you able to fully
  embrace the idea that these are God's gifts in
  you? If not, how can you open your hands wider to
  them?
- How have you seen God use you—uniquely you—in
  your world?

2. Your Personal Voice: Listen to Your Life

Continuing in your journal, move on to identifying your personal voice. Wander through these questions, stopping to answer those that nudge you. Make a note to go back to answer more in the days ahead.

- What events/experiences/education are unique to your life?
- What words or phrases have others used to describe you?
- How would you describe yourself?
- Do you know the meaning of your name? If you don't, look it up. How does this name fit you? What aspects of it leave you cold? How can you grow into it?
- Is there another name you would like to give yourself? What would it be?
- Have you had a nickname given to you? What has been your response to it?
- What are you most proud of in yourself?
- Where have you failed and what have you learned from failure?
- What area of yourself would you like to change?
- Have you taken any of the plethora of personality tests that can help you define and understand your unique voice? If so, what have you learned? If not, which would you like to start with?
- How authentic and true is your voice? To what degree are you the same person in public as you

are in private? Are there certain areas of your being that are more authentic than others? Can you name them? Why do you think this is the case?

- Are you able to speak with your true voice in most circumstances? In what situations do you find your voice censored or even silenced?
- Can you be as intentional about your own personhood as you are about the people and causes and efforts around you? What steps could you take to increase your investment in yourself?
- What can you do that you've never done?
- What energizes you in your everyday life? What activities, relationships, or experiences bring you joy?

3. Personalize Psalm 139

Read through Psalm 139 and insert your own name or the personal pronouns *me, my, mine,* and *I.* Listen to how the meaning deepens! Try this with other scriptures as well.

O LORD, you have examined _____ heart
    and know everything about _____.
You know when _____ sits down or stands up.
    You know _____ thoughts even when _____ is
    far away.
You see _____ when _____ travels
    and when _____ rests at home.
    You know everything _____ does.
You know what _____ is going to say
    even before _____ says it, LORD.

You go before _____ and follow _____.

You place your hand of blessing on _____ head.

Such knowledge is too wonderful for _____,

too great for _____ to understand! (vv. 1–6 NLT)[19]

VESSEL

Beauty in Your Physical Body

To protect our heart, we have learned to lock away our natural God-given beauty by pretending to be the person the world would approve of. . . .

God created us in His image, and the essence of God is beauty; therefore, you and I are beautiful. It is already there; we just need to allow the touch of God to reveal it to us and unleash it.

—Heidi McLaughlin[1]

Growing up, I had a best friend named Barbie. Tall, with a brunette ponytail, bangs, and precise, never-smudged eyeliner, she kept me company for hours and hours and hours. I loved dressing her in her pencil skirts, fur-trimmed jackets, and—the *best* to my sturdy-sneakers-wearing toes—her spiky, slip-on stilettos. Sure, at times I wondered at her form: permanently arched feet; her itsy-bitsy waist, where the joints of her hips allowed effortless splits at the insistence of my eight-year-old fingers; and of course, her cone-shaped breasts that permanently influenced my later dissatisfaction with my own.

In spite of her stereotypical female shape, I didn't see her as perfect so much as pretty. She was a faithful friend, present at my call, compliant to my desires, a willing accomplice to all my imaginings. It was much later, in my teen years and her Malibu phase, that I began to understand the impact created on me and on others by her glamorous ways. Do you realize that a real woman with Barbie's measurements would tally at 39–18–33? She'd also be five-foot-nine and weigh 110 pounds. With these stats for a body, she would not be able to menstruate, would have to crawl on all fours, and would have many medical problems.[2] Poor thing.

Barbie has had a subtle but very real effect on today's girl grown to be a woman: she promised endless possibilities, both in physique and in profession. Whether dressed in the June Cleaver shirtwaist, pearls, and high heels of the late fifties, clad in the beehive and psychedelic print pantsuit of the early sixties, or morphed into Doctor Barbie, Princess Barbie, or Holiday Barbie, Barbie has served as our role model of all things woman. Her multiple variations imply that one beautiful Barbie could never contain all facets of a woman's potential; rather, we needed *more* to express our collective possibilities.

Alas. She meant well—really, she did. Today, staring into her tattoo-lined eyes, we women can experience a deep disappointment, a chasm of unmet expectations about our lives and the vessels through which we live them. What we'd hoped to become—in her image—never grew to be.

Vessel. The word is used of a pot, bowl, jug, pitcher, ewer, basin, and bottle. In a spiritual sense, vessel implies a reception of spiritual influence. Most simply it means "container."

On my bathroom counter sits an array of vessels, each designed to contain a substance so that it can be accessed, used, and enjoyed to its optimum potential. Perfume spritzes from a glass atomizer. Toothpaste oozes from a tube across a brush in a neat line. Kleenex tissues pop up one at a time from a slit, square box. A variety of containers that contain a variety of essences used for a variety of purposes.

A vessel is also that which holds—contains—God's image on this planet. We're talking "body" here, but with terms unaccessorized by stereotypical thinking that can bog us down in body-image quicksand.

As with each of the other places where God's beauty shines in and through us, our vessels require reimaging (*reimagining!*) to God's perspective and intentions. God sees our vessels—every single one of them—as *beauty full.*

Let's break down our view of vessel into four interconnected components: flesh, curve, brain, and muscle. Where do you get stuck in seeing how God sees the container for his being that is your body?

Flesh

At birth my body was too pudgy. "Built-in ruffles!" That's how my mother described my baby thighs. As I grew, my limbs and torso stretched scrawny and remained that way through middle school. Flat. Shapeless. Ever-scuffed knees poked out from my baggy shorts. Eventually I budded—*shock!*—but never to the extent of Barbie. A long season of average followed, in which I lived a bland life of not-enoughness. Today I stare at my middle-age pounds, paunches, and pooches, my folds, creases, and dimples, and wonder what on earth happened. I wouldn't say I've warred with my body the way some women have battled. But I sure get its betrayal of my expectations. My body can be so . . . eeewww! And I haven't even faced serious disease yet.

Oh, the disdain we women hold for our bodies! Pretty much all of us struggle with the flesh component of our vessels. A *Glamour* survey of more than three hundred women of all sizes revealed that, on average, women have thirteen negative body thoughts daily. Nearly one for every waking hour! Ninety-seven percent admitted to having at least one "I hate my body" moment every day.[3] And my, how early such negativity begins! From elementary age on, females aspire to those Barbie-like dimensions as their goal for their own physical development, when in reality, only surgery and starvation can produce such measurements.[4] By the time we reach womanhood, some 80 percent of us are unhappy with our appearances, and more than 10 million suffer from an eating disorder.[5] And my dear Facebook friends are no different. Nearly 46 percent reported that they either don't like or *hate* their bodies, and this makes them unconfident in who they are as women.[6] The things we say to ourselves we would *never* say to others! Ouch.

How did we get this way? Like most topics related to the body, the answer is complicated and multifaceted.

First is the *global* view of body beauty. There's just no way to make everyone everywhere happy with how you look. What is considered lovely in Thailand is very different from what is labeled beautiful in America. Jessica Simpson's 2010 VH1 series, *The Price of Beauty*, charted the degrees to which models venture in order to create what is considered beautiful in their worlds. In Uganda, where large bodies are gorgeous, women spend two months in a "fattening hut" before marriage.[7] Contrastingly, in Paris models can't weigh more than 115 pounds.[8] Thailand values pale complexions, achieved through lightening cream.[9] Japanese women undergo a surgical procedure to produce the exotic "double eyelid" so coveted by their culture.[10] You get the picture.

Such a discovery is not unique to Jessica Simpson's video adventure. Esther Honig, a twenty-four-year-old journalist in Kansas City, Missouri, sent a self-portrait—just her face with her hair pulled back and no makeup—to people in some twenty-seven countries with the single-line instruction, "Hi, my name is Esther Honig . . . make me look beautiful." She has received back Photoshopped images of herself with pink lips and green eye shadow and with no eye makeup whatsoever; with streaked, voluminous, wavy hair and with her whole head covered; with darkened and then lightened skin. In all, Esther processed twenty-seven different versions of herself. She looked at the assorted images and responded, "It's me, but it's not me. It's everyone."[11]

At times the global differentiation of beauty is just plain painful. When she moved to Daegu, South Korea, to teach English as a second language, Ashley Perez expected to find a country where her Cuban/Filipino/Korean-American looks helped her belong. Instead, she was "soul-crushed" to receive such descriptors as "plain face," "tired teacher," and "very, very dark" to account for her larger face and makeup-free, olive complexion. That one in five women ages nineteen to forty-nine has undergone plastic surgery in Korea only underlined her difference and resulting definition as "not beautiful enough to live in South Korea."[12]

These apparent global standards are now shifting as Western media leaks onto other areas of our planet. In Polynesian culture, bigger once meant healthier and stronger. After three years of the introduction of Western media, 74 percent of Fijian teenage girls described themselves as too fat. Those who watched TV three or more nights a week were 30 percent more likely to go on a diet than their peers who watched less.[13]

Our global, media-based culture offers myriad interpretations as to what is and isn't beautiful in bodies. No wonder we struggle so with the flesh of our vessels!

But there is an even greater influence on our views of body beauty, in a core-of-our-being kind of way: the assessment of beauty we inherit from our families and friends of origin. *Thin-heritance* is a phrase coined to express how genetic and environmental views of beauty are passed down from generation to generation. They are, surprisingly, strongly passed through the very beings who somehow know better and mean to do the very opposite: our mothers, our fathers, our siblings, boyfriends, husbands, and various significant others.[14]

The influence of moms is worth pausing over. *People* named Kenyan-raised Academy Award–winner Lupita Nyong'o as

2014's "World's Most Beautiful Woman." Growing up, Lupita didn't think she fit the Hollywood stereotype of beauty. In fact, she defined beauty as "what I saw on television, you know, light skin and long, flowing, straight hair. . . . Subconsciously you start to appreciate those things more than what you possess."[15] Reassessment of her beauty perspective came from her mother. "My mother always said I was beautiful, and I finally believed her at some point."[16]

Marvelous! Mothers can *fix* this body booby trap, right? Yet when I asked Facebook friends about the mother-daughter beauty thing, the response was fascinating. Over 85 percent of you view your daughters as beautiful.[17] Clap! Clap! Clap! But when asked if you believe your mother thought you were beautiful? The response was much lower: only 33 percent received such a message from their moms.[18] Why the difference? Why can we so readily recognize as mothers the beauty in our daughters—and so quickly dismiss from our mothers the beauty in ourselves? Why aren't more of us cut from Lupita's cloth?

There are yet others who affect our views of our flesh— friends, peers, bosses, even strangers who offer some random, but sticky, comment. And oh, the painful results of vessel violation in distorting our body perceptions! The culprits of physical or sexual molestation and abuse—often a family member or close friend—leave confusing definitions of body beauty. Even our levels of career and relationship satisfaction can alter our body thoughts. As one psychologist puts it, "It's all about your body—and absolutely nothing about your body."[19]

A chat about a woman's body can never be complete without

addressing the age issue. You know, what happens when your body rebels and runs renegade—*down*. Sagging breasts, turkey chin, waggly upper arms, wrinkly butt.

We struggle to see our sag as the swag that God sees: "Gray hair is a crown of splendor; it is attained in the way of righteousness" (Proverbs 16:31). (Of course, I'm still covering my gray for the moment.) But the point is made. We diminish the offering of our aging—and eventually terminal—bodies rather than respect the beauty of living that makes them what they are.

In an essay titled "The Aunties," middle-aged Anne Lamott's twinkly-eyed embrace of her upper thighs pokes great fun at our disdain for elderly vessels. A tiny excerpt:

> I got my suit on and waddled down to the beach.
>
> I was not wearing a cover-up, not even a T-shirt. I had decided I was going to take my thighs and butt with me proudly wherever I went. I decided, in fact, on the way to the beach that I would treat them as if they were beloved elderly aunties, the kind who did embarrassing things at the beach like roll their stockings into tubes around their ankles, but whom I was proud of because they were so great in every *real and important* way.[20]

Gotta love the way Anne learned to love "the aunties"! So what if just a few pages over she sheepishly realized that she was a bit exposed and covered back up? She embraced her baggy beauty, as I hope all of us grow to do.

The forces that shape and diminish our perceptions of our

vessels' flesh as unfavorable are unending: global, cultural, familial, age. All pretty much negative, negative, negative.

In order to see our vessels through God's perception, we'll need a kind of vessel vaccination against the negativity that has been layered over our bodies! It's coming. Keep reading.

But first, on to the next vessel component—smooth sailing for some, a hot mess for others.

Curve

In sixth grade I was a bit behind the curve. My nubile nipples had begun to emerge ever so faintly, but surely not enough to require the wiring and elastic of a full-fledged brassiere. (Good grief, I just had to look up how to spell the thing.) That's what my mother called the contraption, and I was in no hurry to try them on. When I started my period (*Horrors!—on the first day of middle school!*), she wanted to take me to dinner to celebrate my "becoming a woman" and go brassiere shopping. Ugh!

And yet . . .

There were other girls—*initiates?*—of my age who were wearing bras. When they leaned forward at their desks, stretching the thin fabric of their white shirts taut, *everyone* could see they'd been inaugurated into the society of maturity. I wanted in as well.

My not-quite-readiness led me to a pseudo-solution. I wore a full slip under a light pink blouse. I figured if I stretched forward at my desk, the straps would give the appearance of a bra, and I'd be "in" without being "in" (a bra). My plan worked brilliantly—until between classes, when admiring my slip/shirt in the restroom mirror, I realized a strap had broken. While nothing was amiss from the back view of me, the front right side of me—the front right *nipple* side of me—was visible straight through my shirt. I was mortified!

Such a recollection might seem a silly segue into the "curve" part of our vessels, but sexuality is completely rooted in childhood and then shaped from childhood into adulthood. Every girl remembers such a moment, right?

While I've never inhabited what could be described as a curvaceous body nor described myself as a super sexy lady, I've come—slowly—to embrace the reality of my sexuality and the gift it brings me in this world. Oh, the discovery of an ability to turn a head, just because I'm a girl! The amazing way my husband admires what I'd rather hide away. And surprisingly, the adventure of bringing *all* of me before God in enjoyment, realizing there is nothing hidden from his sight or his delight in my womanly being.

Many women struggle on one or the other end of the curve spectrum: shut-down sexuality or overexpressive sexuality. Shut-down women tend to bury their curves. Among the millions of women assailed by eating disorders is the amazing author and blogger Emily Wierenga. She wrote, "I was nine years old when I tried to starve away my curves. I tried to starve away the parts of me that made me a woman."[21] But it's not just "going thin" that hides our discomfort with our curves. Today nearly 36 percent of all women ages twenty and over and about 32 percent of women ages twenty to thirty-nine are obese.[22] On the other end of the spectrum is the overexpressive woman, who acts out her sexuality in suggestive, come-and-get-me clothing, and measures her value by sexual interactions.

Why we end up on one end or the other of the spectrum is complex, including issues like divorce, abandonment, adoption, illness, addiction, sheltering or inappropriate parenting, and sexual or other abuse. Women wounded in the sexual arena may starve away or cover up in shut-down sexuality, or they may act out in overexpression in an effort to gain or regain control over it.

Most of us don't feel good about our curves. When we don't feel good about our bodies, we don't enjoy our sexualities.[23] But God made us sexual beings.

Then there's the exception: a woman who sees her curve as lovely, even if it's mismatched to a stereotypical standard of perfection. Like self-proclaimed "curvy Canadian" model Elly Mayday. Just as she was about to sign with a New York modeling agency, she was diagnosed with a rare form of ovarian cancer. After surgery and chemotherapy, Elly continues to model lingerie for a company in Canada, baring her scars and bald head with seventy-four thousand Facebook supporters cheering her on. Elly's goal in her transparency is to help women see beyond the stereotypical sexed-up woman in the glossies. In an interview with ABC News, Elly said, "In the lingerie industry, it's not something you do. . . . It's all about long hair and big breasts and arched backs. But it's important to show what real women look like underneath their clothes. Most people have some issue they are dealing with."[24] While I have no idea if Elly knows the God who made her and loves her so, I find in her attitude a refreshing embrace of how God sees us.

We get so mixed up here! I love the title of a book by Dan Allender and Tremper Longman III: *God Loves Sex*.[25] Yup! Our sexuality is part of God's created purpose; it's not the result of the fall. "God saw all that he had made, and it was very good" (Genesis 1:31). Yes, sexual desire has been corrupted by the fall (*Hisssssss!*), but we need to understand that when God says we were created *good*, he included our sexuality in that pronouncement. We can take what we see as a lack of "curve appeal" to God and invite him to help us see ourselves as he does.

Brain

I finished the interview, and my host wrapped the segment with a heartfelt plea for prayer and provided a phone number for viewers to call. Done. I had felt God spread his offering through the message he had guided me to share in this television taping. It was a *good* moment.

When I returned to the green room to gather my purse and head out, a staffer stopped me and sheepishly asked if he could record a side bit for the web. Just a few easy questions, he promised.

Well, sure, I thought. I was used to putting my desires in neutral when it came to ministry. When I was booked for an engagement, I had learned to flex my schedule and plans to God's leading and the needs of the venue I served.

I sat in front of the microphone, and my host fired off the

question, "Can you name the twelve disciples?" It was a game-show kind of moment, and like many contestants I've seen botch their slots, I went blank. To be honest, even if I had been prepared, I'm not sure I would have known the names of the twelve disciples without opening the Bible. I mumbled something like, "Matthew, Mark, Luke, and John." Oh wait—those were the Gospel writers. Were they all among the Twelve? I sputtered, "And Judas. And then there was Paul. And Nathanael." Where had that anointing gone? I felt so *duh* . . .

It surely wasn't the first time. So many of my efforts have been offered with a wince—would I be "found out" this time? In my finals in graduate school, I'd been asked to explain a book of the Bible—a teeny tiny book in the Old Testament. That I'd never read. Oh my.

Today I still doubt the adequacy of my brain. Such a stigma has been nicknamed *imposter syndrome*—the phenomenon where, despite evidence of competence, we're convinced we're frauds and don't deserve the success we've achieved.[26] Oh, I'm whip-smart when it comes to emotional intelligence. I can intuit a feeling or mood or need before I even enter a room. And my mind for movie trivia is stupidly smart. (Wait—isn't that an oxymoron? Oh dear, there's the word *moron*!) But whatever I know that I know is eclipsed by what I'm afraid I don't know or have forgotten now that I'm older.

My husband gets mad at me when I talk (write) this way. He knows I'm smart and wants to stomp on such diminishing self-think like he would a cockroach in Texas. A lot of women downplay their intelligence like this.

Not every woman struggles with intelligence, to be sure. Some women cling to their mortarboards like life preservers, trusting degrees, titles, and publications to define their identities. One of my cohorts in ministry confesses, "I have the need to be the smart girl. And often it does bring affirmation. But who I am is so much bigger and more significant than that—when I look inside and realize it."

The thing is, women *are* smart. New Zealand-based researcher James Flynn found that women have surpassed men in IQ test scores for the first time. He attributes such performance to the effects of modernity, where women are asked to juggle domestic and workplace realities.[27]

In addition, women are uniquely smart, carrying abilities desperately needed in our world in its current season of history. The *Daily Mail* reported on several findings from the journal *Proceedings of the National Academy of Sciences*:

> Women's and men's brains are wired in fundamentally different ways. . . .
>
> Men generally have more connections within each hemisphere and between the front and back of the brain.
>
> In women the stronger connections usually run from side to side, between the left and right hemispheres.
>
> In essence, what this means is that men are more logical and better at coordination and spatial awareness. Women are more intuitive, have greater "emotional intelligence" and better memories for words and faces.[28]

In a day when emotional intelligence seals deals, a woman's emotional braininess is vital. Buckholdt Associations reported,

"Both men and women have emotional intelligence . . . but each gender has a significantly different Emotional Intelligence profile. Women have much stronger interpersonal skills than their male counterparts but men have significantly higher sense of self and independence."[29]

We need to embrace the reality that what our world needs is what we have packed in our brains as women—each of us individually and women together.

Muscle

Just recently has this fourth element of vessel begun to be accepted in our feminine bodies. Oh sure, a few Olympians have mastered their muscles into success with a clear embrace of their bodies. Figure skater Kristi Yamaguchi. Gymnast Gabby Douglas. Swimmer Amy Van Dyken (and now as a paraplegic—wow!).

I would have to agree that applying the term of *muscle* to my feminine being is a new one for me. When was the first time I realized the power of my body? Perhaps when I was a teenage cheerleader.

I think back to my one and only 10K race, the Bolder Boulder, which takes place here in Colorado. I was, what, maybe forty? I had never run more than a mile. But our small group from church entered together, and competitive as I've shared that I was (and am), I trained.

The day of the race, I ended up going pretty much solo. We all did, as our bodies and paces were unique. When I crested the last hill, one man from our small group was in front of me, and he slowed to check on how I was doing. And brilliantly, he invested his best coaching abilities in cheering me on. I pumped my arms and swelled my lungs in stride to his commands, and—*bam!*—I finished in less than an hour. His coaching led me to be better than I had ever imagined I could be. I sensed the power of my muscle for the first time as an adult woman. It felt good.

Musician P!nk reveals her "secret" to becoming comfortable with her physique:

> I was a gymnast for eight years, starting when I was 4 years old. . . . So instead of thinking, "Am I skinny? What does my body look like?" I grew up thinking, "Am I fast enough? How can I use my body?" I'm a person who could always lose a couple here and there, but I would rather be strong than bony.[30]

One American study reveals that female body builders like the way their bodies look more than other women. A London University study confirms the finding, showing that athletic women have a more positive body image and appreciate their muscular body shapes.[31]

Perhaps we're a bit GI-Jane-come-lately when it comes to embracing the muscle component of our vessels, but women today are starting to see something strong, where in prior generations only a "gentle and quiet spirit" would do.

Four components together form our unique vessels, and God sees each of them as beautiful. Likely you feel more confident about one of these aspects than the others. Taking some time to identify which—and why—can strengthen your overall vessel image. Once you do that work, can you invite God into the troublesome element?

Vessel Reimaged

Vessel. Container. That which holds something—something physical and also something spiritual as well.

The Bible is pretty clear that in addition to housing our own unique personalities (voices), our bodies were created to contain the Spirit of God himself: "Do you not know that your bodies are temples of the Holy Spirit, who is in you, whom you have received from God? You are not your own; you were bought at a price. Therefore honor God with your bodies" (1 Corinthians 6:19–20). The word *temple* here is multifaceted. In the Old Testament, it referred to the physical temple where God's people gathered to worship. But in the New Testament, Jesus used this word of his own mortal body, and Paul employed it to describe the body of believers, both individual and corporate.[32]

While Paul's definition of the body in this passage focused on sexual immorality—honoring God with your body by participating in appropriate sexual expression—he offered a helpful insight on the overall purpose of our vessels: to contain God's presence in us and in our world. God created our vessels so that he could inhabit them—all aspects of our beings—with us. Flesh. Curve. Brain. Muscle. God himself lives within our vessels when they're the size of figs in our mothers' wombs and when

99

they've been stretched to sagging simply by living the life we've been given.

Such a thing leaves me still somehow "naked and ashamed." God, with me, in my vessel? I come unhinged at the thought. In my puny understanding, it's as if the supernatural and the natural just can't coexist. Cannot. At least not in *my* ugly natural.

But this really is what God did. Unashamedly. John wrote, "The Word became flesh and made his dwelling among us" (John 1:14). God put himself in a vessel. The Word—Jesus, God's very best expression of himself to us—became *flesh*. That's the term for a physical body made up of flesh, curve, brain, and muscle. And God made his dwelling among us, meaning he took up residence in our world in a vessel just like ours. A temporary tent of sorts—again, like ours.

God formed himself in the womb of a woman's vessel. God scrunched himself through her opening and was born in our world in the vessel of a baby. God formed objects through the vessel hands of a carpenter, and he walked with the vessel feet of a man. God expressed himself in the vessel of flesh, curve, brain, and muscle of a human. The vessel of Jesus' body was nailed to a cross and raised up to die in my place and in yours. Then Jesus' dead vessel was placed in a tomb where, after three days, God raised it from death to life while *still* containing God in a vessel.

Yet the concept of God in flesh—in *our* flesh—gives us the willies. Barbara Brown Taylor cataloged our human discomfort with this stupefying mystery:

> I am not sure when Christian tradition lost confidence in the body, but I have some guesses. Although Jesus was a Jew,

many of his earliest interpreters were Greeks, who divided body and soul in ways that he did not. Descartes did not help matters by opposing nature and reason in his philosophy. Then along came the Protestant Reformation, with its deep suspicion of physical pleasure, followed by Freud's dark insights into human sexuality. Add to that the modern scientific reduction of the body to biological matter, overlaid by Victoria's Secret ads, and it is small wonder that so many of us are uncomfortable in our flesh.[33]

If God deigned to reveal himself to us through the vessel of a human body, and he was perfect, can we learn to see our vessels—made in his image—as filled with beauty? If God chose to house himself on this planet within our vessels, can we embrace that we are *beauty full* because we contain the *beauty full* One? As Sarah Young echoed God's heart, "All true beauty reflects some of who I am."[34]

I turn the pages of the Bible back from 1 Corinthians 6 and John 1 to Psalm 45:11: "Let the king be enthralled by your beauty; honor him, for he is your lord." This Psalm is interpreted as a wedding hymn—perhaps used in the marriage of a man and woman—but because of the exalted language, the words are more often seen as messianic. As such, this verse depicts the marriage of the body of Christ, and individual believers within the church, to Jesus. Us!

Read these words again: "Let the king be enthralled by your beauty; honor him, for he is your lord."

That's how God, the king, sees us: *beauty full.* He is *enthralled* by our beauty, and we are to let him be enthralled for our lifetimes. From the beginning of our days as dependent children on through our robust youth and into our declining health, God invites us to wed our view of our bodies to his enthralled view. In Song of Songs, the scriptures take this even further, embellishing our beauty into the fullest expression of vessel: flesh, curve, brain, muscle.

You know what's really interesting? So many women report that the moment in their lives when they felt most beautiful was on their wedding day: a moment when the negativity slid back, they were chosen and cherished just as they were, and their husbands vowed to do so forever.[35]

But we forget. And excuse. And diminish. And rationalize. And go negative.

God wants us to remember, even if we haven't ever stood with another human at an altar of commitment. Even if the vow was broken. Even if we have so flushed the hope of cherishing our bodies that to resurrect it is beyond our comprehension. God wants us to remember how he sees us—that "God loves flesh and blood, no matter what kind of shape it is in."[36]

God wants us to remember how much he loves us. And God wants us to see our physical bodies the way he sees them: as containers he created for us to inhabit with him.

Henri Nouwen gently persuaded us to come "home" to our bodies:

> You have never felt completely safe in your body. But God wants to love you in all that you are, spirit and body.

Increasingly, you have come to see your body as an enemy that has to be conquered. But God wants you to befriend your body so that it can be made ready for the Resurrection. [*As the Bride of Christ!*] When you do not fully own your body, you cannot claim it for an everlasting life.[37]

God invites each of us, as his bride, to make vessel vows to see our bodies the way he sees them. Flesh, curve, brain, muscle—each is beauty full because he sees each as a container perfectly designed to hold his essence. He wants us to embrace what he embraced when "the Word became flesh and made his dwelling among us." How about it? Let's roll out our mats, open our doors, and welcome God home!

Becoming Beauty Full You

1. Evaluate Your Mirrors
Margot Starbuck startles us into honesty about the extreme level of our self-judgment with her personal list of irrelevant judges in her life. See if her observations jumpstart your perspective.

Ten People Whose Judgment About
My Body Is Entirely Irrelevant
1. People who will evaluate what I'm wearing in church
2. People who see me wearing unflattering Lycra while doing cardio
3. People who are younger than me

4. People who are older than me

5. People my age

6. The mail carrier

7. People leaner than me

8. People chunkier than me

9. Men

10. Women[38]

2. Mirror Messages

Place sticky notes with the messages God says are true about your vessel on every mirror in your house, car, and purse. Train your eye to see the truth talk on the sticky note rather than the "mess" in the mirror. *Hello, Beauty Full! You are loved! You are fearfully and wonderfully made! Love God back by loving your body!*

When you notice some inevitable body "bump," whether as small as a blemish or as large as cancer, train your eye to love your vessel by seeing it the way God sees it. *Even here my body is good. In this weakness God can bring me strength.*

3. Dear Daughter

Make sure your daughter knows that her body is beautiful by loving your own body. Refrain from self-criticism; instead, let her see you care for your body and accept those things you see as flaws. See your body the way God sees it, and model this image before her.

Then, help your daughter learn to see the beauty she houses in her body. Alexandra Kuykendall, mother of four daughters, shares five messages to pass along.

1. *Your joy is beautiful.* "You have a beautiful smile." "Your eyes twinkle when you're thinking about that." "It makes me happy to see you so happy." There is a radiance about people who are enjoying the moment. We can teach girls that with the ways we affirm them in those moments of joy.

2. *Your talents are beautiful.* "You did that puzzle all by yourself? You are so good at that!" "Wow! You are fast on your bike!" "I think that drawing is lovely. Can you tell me about it?" God makes us each unique, [and] there is no reason we shouldn't point out girls' natural abilities to encourage them to live into who God made them to be. They don't have to be delicate talents either (think fine arts) they just need to be uniquely hers and we need to be genuinely interested in them.

3. *Your heart is beautiful.* "Thank you for that hug. That helped cheer me up." "That was so thoughtful when you brought your sister your bear." "Great job including everyone when you were at school today. I can tell it made your friends feel special." God's heart is for us to treat each other well. Beauty in action is certainly attractive. Catch her doing things right.

4. *Your thoughts are beautiful.* "What did you think of that story?" "I've never thought of it that way." "That is a great idea!" From her opinions to her ponderings, you are getting insights into who she is. When you affirm her questions or insights you are letting her know she has something valuable to contribute to discussions and the world. That her ideas matter.

5. *Your presence is beautiful.* "It's so good to see you." "I'm glad you're here." "I've missed you." Are my fallbacks when I greet a girl and nothing else comes to mind. These are all ways to let a girl know her very existence is a gift to others and you're glad she is around. This speaks right into why she is valuable. She is valuable because she was created and bears God's image. It's so simple and indeed beautiful.[39]

4. Mirror Prayer

Barbara Brown Taylor challenges us to take a deep breath, remove our clothes, and pray naked in front of a full-length mirror.

God loves flesh and blood, no matter what kind of shape it is in. Whether you are sick or well, lovely or irregular, there comes a time when it is vitally important for your spiritual health to drop your clothes, look in the mirror, and say, "Here I am. This is the body-like-no-other that my life has shaped. I live here. This is my soul's address.[40]

seven

WOMB

Beauty in Your Creative Purpose

> The Victorian woman became her ovaries, as
> today's woman has become her "beauty."
>
> —Naomi Wolf[1]

I've never given birth. I've never even been pregnant. When my date—who became my fiancé and eventually my husband—first told me he wouldn't be able to have children biologically, I instinctively turned away from my possible new normal to consider his ongoing reality. I was stunned at the ordeal of cancer that Evan had survived. At twenty-four—*my*! I listened as he shared that he was "cured" and that he would have a very normal life as a man, sans biological children. The spiritual depth with which he shared his life sentence called to me, deep unto deep. Within a few hours, I seemingly grew gills and submerged, tandem-diving with him into the place he'd learned to call home—a new world I never knew existed. A world bordered with words like *barren*, *childless*, and *infertile*. While my body would continue to form and shed eggs for several decades to come, my womb would yawn empty—forever.

Knowing full well that the only path to parenting for us would be adoption, Evan and I applied just weeks after our wedding. We had done our research and discovered the process was famously arduous. We didn't want to wait any longer than the projected average of four to five years. At first it didn't seem so bad. After all, like most newlyweds, we weren't in a giant rush to become parents. We liked each other and enjoyed our time together moving forward in life as a couple.

A year or two passed, and we waited. And waited. I had never really cared all that much about having kids. In some ways I had already plowed such ground in raising my younger brother in my messy and broken first family. But after the third and into the fourth year, I grew more than tired of waiting. The whole ordeal was like being dilated to a nine for years! *I wanted a baby!*

I witnessed other births; in fact, I was blessed and better because I was invited into the actual process with two friends. With one I was a coach—though in my naive condition, I had little to offer other than prayer and presence. With the other, I held her kindergarten daughter, who wrapped herself like a monkey around the tree of my waist and buried her head in my shoulder while her mama panted and pushed. In both hospital rooms, birthing brought forth beautiful life with undeniable awe.

Christmas came as Evan and I completed our fourth year of waiting. Every couple in the adoption study group had received their baby, except us. Strains from "What Child Is This?"

haunted me. I set up a special Christmas tree, tying pink and blue ribbons on its branches. Daily I paused before its evergreen boughs to beg God for a baby by Christmas. I named it my "Hope for the Baby" tree. From the well within my being, a wound called out to be named. A grief. Years earlier, free-falling in love, I'd nonchalantly discarded my ability to reproduce biologically. *Adoption would be fine!* I was not in the least regretful of the man I had chosen. I loved—and still love—Evan with all my heart. But as the months passed, and my arms remained empty, the loss in my womb called out to me for attention.

Finally, the next spring—nearly five years after we "conceived"—the hope of receiving a child into our family through adoption culminated. Easter weekend emerged with news of our baby coming. At last! Our daughter was brought forth from the womb of another and entrusted into our arms, christening us parents. In the womb of my heart, love was born. Then nearly three years later, the incarnate miracle of adoption repeated, this time with a baby boy, our son.

Over the next decade or so, I mothered and worked and lived. The topic of my womb sat silent and unseen. What womb? The monthly reminder of its unmet potential annoyingly continued, but I doubt I felt much different about that than any other woman, fertile or infertile. Ironically, when my teenage daughter presented herself suddenly pregnant, and I rallied to become all things mother/husband/teacher/mentor to her impending motherhood, my own menstruation began to ebb. I stood at her head as an emergency C-section yielded a beautiful baby, whom she would relinquish through adoption. Our hearts and souls emptied out our love, and oddly, for a time my daughter and I shared our wombs' apparent betrayal. Mine: infertile and empty. Hers: fertile but with no fruit to show for her efforts.

Later my daughter became pregnant again and carried another baby through and into life, becoming a permanent mother and making me a permanent grandmother. I was present when he made his entrance from the dark of her inner world into the messy, noisy, blinding light of this one. Again, I embraced the miracle with awe.

Life continued. I parented and grandparented and worked and lived. My monthly flow ceased. The next family pregnancies cruelly slid from life into death before ever emerging, leaving further hollowness in our hearts. One, an eerie, silent birth of stillness, wracked us all with pain. So much effort with—again—no fruit! A life so desperately desired—vanished away!

Nearly twenty years before, I had been tapped to lead MOPS International. It had been an ironic placement for never-pregnant me to head up a mothering organization. Yet I had watched God grow me and MOPS and millions of moms through his call on my life there. In my latter years of leadership, something began shifting inside me. An "expectancy" for something new, something of my own, rose up urgently within me. It seemed my inner being was speaking to my outer world. It dawned on me that while I'd served so long and arduously at MOPS, in a way I'd adopted MOPS as well. I was not involved in its fifteen-year historic beginning. Instead, I was handed an already-formed baby to raise and then launch. Even at MOPS, I was barren.

Just recently, I rediscovered a long-buried reality. I want to be pregnant. I still want to give birth. Old-woman me wants to be belly out, waddling with a womb filled with wonder.

What does this barren status mean about who I am, about my contribution on this planet as a woman? I've raised children from other women's wombs as my very own. I know that totally counts. I've brought to maturity an organization that had been conceived by others. That counts too. But how does God see such an apparently barren womb as *beauty full*? And what do I do with such a thing?

Bearing children changes a woman. It widens her world and multiplies her heart offering. No doubt. But not bearing children is equally impactful. Surgeons in Sweden have transplanted uteruses in nine infertile women in hopes of them becoming pregnant.[2] One woman confessed to me that childlessness is the most crippling factor in how she views herself as a woman: "I am childless. I see this often as a defect of my character. Like, God doesn't think I would make a good mother. Like, I'm too evil."[3]

Ouch. So very "hissssssssy."

The F(ertile) Word

While at times painful to those of us who have not born babies, there is something undeniably *female* about fertility. As little girls, we cart around our dollies, play house, and serve imaginary tea—all while gluing our gazes on the Mommy Prize. Our wombs seem central to our offering as women.

Think back over some of the most historic wombs in the

Bible. Eve (whose name means "full of life") conceived and bore the first babies ever made—Cain and then Abel. Sarah's wrinkly placenta sustained the line of Abraham. Tamar (who posed as a prostitute to trick her father-in-law to sleep with her), Hannah (whose infertile womb first defined her as lacking and then finally, with her son Samuel, as adequate), Rahab (harlot spy and mother of Boaz), Ruth (foreigner), Bathsheba (adulteress with King David)—all kinds of wombs wind through the genealogy of Jesus in Matthew 1. John the Baptist, who would prepare the way for the Messiah, leaped within—and then from—an old woman's womb. And God incarnated himself in the virginal womb of a young teenage girl.

A woman's worth—honorable and dishonorable—has been expressed through her womb for millennia. While it is undeniable, it is also elusive and sometimes troubling.

As one who is female without being fertile, I know.

But hey—I know *lots* of women who are childless, and they seem perfectly happy to me! One accompanies her husband around the globe and supports his platformed ministry. Another heads up a large business. Another quietly administrates her family's entrepreneurial efforts and gives gobs of money to amazing kingdom causes. We are no more women if we give birth and no less women if we don't. No more female if we adopt and become mothers and no less if we remain childless.

Emily Wierenga mused, "Apart from all of the gender and theological debates, what does it mean to be this unique creature who weaves humanity in her abdomen and nurses infants through her breasts and speaks life with her eyes, her mouth, her hands? What does it mean to be this in today's world? And why does it feel so lonely?"[4]

Women are womb-defined. And womb stuff is messy.

What if we expand our understanding of the concept of womb? What if we come to know that while the potential to birth is central to our vocation, calling, and contribution as women, this one expression does not—cannot—contain our complete offering? What if we see in the hollow within not just a space for creating physical life but also a mysterious interior source of creating contributions of all kinds? What if we see a womb as a place of *purposed creation*, even vocation?

Counselor Jayne Spear suggested a fuller perspective about our womb's purpose when she wrote,

> In addition to a physical space, as any woman can testify, there exists a deeper opening, a holy place where we hear our truest echo. In this place we make room for others to nurture, hold and pass on our wisdom. This space, uniquely feminine, is godlike in its essence. Like him, who out of the space inside himself brought forth life, he designed us to become, in addition to many things, *mothers.*[5]

"In addition to many things." Hmmm.

While ardent mothers like Susanna Wesley, who birthed nineteen children (among them John and Charles, the founders of the Methodist church), abound in the legacy of their physical wombs, women have contributed widely in other areas. Sacagawea guided Lewis and Clark in their exploration of the western United States.

Along with her husband, William, Catherine Booth founded the Salvation Army. Amelia Earhart piloted solo almost around the world. Malala Yousafzai stood for peace and against terrorism, winning the 2014 Nobel Peace Prize.

Yes, women are divinely designed to be mothers, and when we do mother, we spend about one-fourth of our lives in active mothering. But women who are mothers are more than mothers. And children are not the only offering women are capable of creating.

God designed women to be mothers—and more. God designed women to make babies—and to make more. The womb is a space of creation—of others and of ourselves.

Take Mary, the mother of Jesus. Surely it is her physical womb that expressed her vocation: to bear the Messiah. Yet her physical womb extended her calling beyond what was formed *within* her to a spiritual womb that conceived and gave birth to how she herself *externally* followed him as Lord. Her relative, Elizabeth, six months pregnant with John the Baptist, proclaimed, "Blessed is she who has believed that the Lord would fulfill his promises to her!" (Luke 1:45). Elizabeth spoke of the miraculous conception of Jesus in Mary's womb, but surely her words also prophesied all that God would do through Mary's obedience in her lifetime to come. Beyond the physical birth of the Messiah, Mary "treasured up all these things and pondered them in her heart" over the years (Luke 2:19).

Thus, she created and birthed forth acts of trust and beauty from her spiritual womb: raising the Christ child, dedicating him in the temple, accompanying him on his first miracle of turning water into wine, standing inside and outside rooms as he taught, bending at the foot of the cross, and marveling at the empty tomb.

When we grasp that a woman's womb can create both physical *and* spiritual contributions in our world, suddenly *all* women are included! A woman's physical womb is a cocreational place where she is called to participate with God in the birthing of baby people. And a woman's soul womb is a cocreational space where she is called to participate in the rebirthing of people to become children of God. For some women, our vocations will include birthing or adopting children. For some they won't. But for all of us, our womb expression will play out in our participation with God in his creative purposes in our world.

Womb Work

So how do we see our womb vocations as God does? How do we know what he wants our wombs to create?

Traditionally, the concept of vocation has taken on a connotation as coming from outside of us. Like Mary being visited by an angel in Luke 1:31: "You will conceive and give birth to a son, and you are to call him Jesus." Like God's appearance to the apostle Paul on the road to Damascus in Acts 9:5–6: "I am Jesus, whom you are persecuting. . . . Now get up and go into the city, and you will be told what you must do." Or like when Daniel was called to interpret God's handwriting on the wall before the Babylonian king Belshazzar in Daniel 5.

But in real life, God's call to vocation doesn't come so

externally for most of us. Angels never appeared to announce just when I would receive my children through adoption. Jesus hasn't shown up at my bedside to give me instructions for my day. And my walls are smudged with fingerprints and dog smear (that's what I call the oil of their skin dirtying my taupe walls). Unless I stencil some Hobby Lobby quotation over my mantel, you're not going to find words from God inked on my plaster.

Yet we still expect this miraculous, vision-seeing, voice-hearing, *Song of Bernadette*-esque call from God. Sure, there have been moments in my life when God has woven scripture and prayer and comments from people into divine leading to do this or say that or go there. But such instances are rare.

Early on in his own life, Parker J. Palmer latched on to the belief that "vocation, or calling, comes from a voice external to ourselves, a voice of moral demand that asks us to become some-one we are not yet—someone different, someone better, someone just beyond our reach." As he matured, he realized, "That con-cept of vocation is rooted in a deep distrust of selfhood, in the belief that the sinful self will always be 'selfish' unless corrected by external forces of virtue."

And then—*bam!*—he discovered as an older, wiser soul, "Vocation does not come from a voice 'out there' calling me to become something I am not. It comes from a voice 'in here' call-ing me to be the person I was born to be, to fulfill the original selfhood given me at birth by God."[6]

Read that again, and notice the italics I've added: "Vocation does not come from a voice *'out there'* calling me to become something I am not. It comes from a voice *'in here'* calling me to be the person I was *born* to be, to fulfill the original selfhood *given me at birth by God.*"

Fuller clarity of our vocations comes as we look within to who we are and how God sees our creative purposes in our wombs. Understanding our vocations and callings as internally revealed frees us within our individual circumstances. God designed every woman's *beauty full* womb. He placed within women the creative space to become moms—and more. Our vocations may include mothering (physically or through adoption) or not. But all women will create and give life somehow.

Go back to Eve in her conception of the first baby ever born: "Adam made love to his wife Eve, and she became pregnant and gave birth to Cain" (Genesis 4:1). Clearly, the creative purpose of Eve's womb was to form the first son. But look at the rest of verse 1: "She said, 'With the help of the LORD I have brought forth a man.'" As well, the creative purpose of Eve's womb included the formation of *man*. Every man. Every woman. Humankind. From within her physical womb, God brought forth Eve's calling, her vocation as the mother of the first son ever born. And from within her spiritual womb, God brought forth Eve's vocation as the mother of all of life.

With the help of the Lord, what will you bring forth? Both everyday and expert folks have offered a variety of definitions for vocation. See which might best resonate with your understanding of the work to which God has called you.

Vocation is . . .

- "one's entire life lived in response to God's voice."[7]
- "do[ing] anything that pleases you . . . and belong[ing] to me [God]."[8]
- "the work a person is called to by God. . . . The place God calls you to is the place where your deep gladness and the world's deep hunger meet."[9]
- "something [you] can't not do, for reasons [you're] unable to explain to anyone else and don't fully understand [yourself] but that are nonetheless compelling."[10]
- The thing you, and only you, can do.

Richard Rohr suggested, "The first half of life is about creating a container. The second half is about deciding what contents to put in it."[11]

Together with God, I am giving birth to another me. He is inviting me to let that be my work. And God is working in you as well. Whether barren of children or as fruitful as the Old Woman Who Lived in a Shoe. Whether inside or outside the home. Whether in a paychecked effort or one of volunteer labor. Whether in relationship with others or in solo endeavors. God sees your womb as beauty full because he sees the creative purposes for which he has constructed you.

With the help of the Lord, what will you bring forth?

Becoming Beauty Full You

1. Mother Womb

What is the current state of your physical womb? How does this condition affect your view of your value and ability to participate in God's purposes in your world?

If you have already had or decide to have children, you may discover a tearing among your priorities. The spiritual creativity you long for may seem dormant. Later, as your child-rearing responsibilities ebb, your womb will create in other areas. Your work will focus on a rebirth of a new you: wiser, quieter, deeper, calmer.

2. Womb Questions

If you're uncertain as to just what you are called to contribute on this planet, consider these questions:

- What brings you deep gladness?
- What passing thoughts have you had regarding engagement in God's kingdom?
- What is God saying to you these days about your calling?
- Is there any place where you are resisting or have lost touch with who you are?
- Where are you wrestling with God and needing assurance of his presence with you?[12]

3. Everyday Womb

Often we make spiritual work too spiritual. We dress up our

real desires into Sunday-best intentions and try to baptize them into being.

What do you love to do? Do you love to write? Write. Read? Read. Serve? Serve. Teach, give, lead, host parties, listen, paint? Doing that thing may actually be your womb at work.

The relationship God wants us to have with him is *ask*. He loves to give us the desires of our heart.

4. Call: The Now, the New, the Next

A calling to Jesus is twofold. On the one hand, we are called away from something—a certain "now" in our days: Boats. Nets. Fish. Tax collecting. Religion. Sin. On the other hand, a calling is about approaching something "new": Jesus. His voice. His ways. His purposes.

In addition, calling is ongoing. There is always a "next." What's your "now," and how might God be asking you to leave it for your "new"? How is God stepping into your "new" and beckoning you toward your "next"?

5. Unexpected Womb

Into most of our lives comes an unplanned pregnancy of sorts. Sometimes literally—as a teen or single woman or well-intentioned family planner. Often the expected appears in circumstances we never imagined. We find ourselves living lives of contribution in areas we'd never foreseen visiting, much less settling down in permanently.

In her amazing essay "Welcome to Holland," Emily Perl Kingsley describes one such unexpected womb world. She likens the experience of raising a child with special needs to setting out for a fabulous Italian vacation but landing in Holland instead: the location is still pretty and interesting and offers much to discover, but the language, food, and geography are completely different than what you antici- pated. You must adapt in order to embrace.[13]

A different tale with a similar principle comes from the bestselling book *The Alchemist*, by Paulo Coelho. In the exchange with the mentoring alchemist, the apprentice boy asks,

> "And what went wrong when other alchemists tried to make gold and were unable to do so?"
>
> "They were looking only for gold," his companion an- swered. "They were seeking the treasure of their Personal Legend, without wanting actually to live out the Personal Legend."[14]

God may allow the unexpected in our lives. In such a season, our response is to embrace what he brings to our wombs. Consider finding a counselor to serve as a guide in your new world, or join a small group and discover some traveling companions.

eight

SCAR

Beauty in Your Painful Story

You are imperfect, permanently and inevitably
flawed. And you are beautiful.

—Amy Bloom[1]

The butterfly flitted in and out of the panda-faced pansies.
Stained-glass wings worked rhythmically as it lighted and then
launched from petal to petal. To my four-year-old eyes, it was
a magic being promising fairy-tale dreams come true. I had to
have it.

I raced from our backyard, through the garage, and into our
kitchen. "Mommy!" I screeched, eager for her help in catching
my unicorn-like discovery. But Mother wasn't in the kitchen. No
one was there. No matter—I would catch it myself! There was no
time to lose. I pulled open the bottom drawer and scoured the
various containers for a suitable trap. There! A mason jar, with a
lid that actually matched! Perfect! Grabbing its shiny offering in

my pudgy hands, I raced back out the door, through the garage, toward the backyard flower bed where I'd last seen my prey. At the last second, though, I missed the raised step from garage to backyard and tripped, sending myself sprawling on the concrete patio. Beneath me, the jar smashed to glass bits under my right wrist, and an ugly slash of flesh spurted blood.

I remember the ride to the emergency room, my father driving, my mother bundling me in my great-grandmother's blue-and-white quilt that she tore from my bed. I remember her holding me in her arms in the front seat with my arm pressed tight in a washrag. I remember a momentary glimpse when I turned my arm over and stared at the gash—a white island of flesh floating in a sea of blood—before my mother clamped her grip once again. I remember the gurney where I lay and cried with all my might, while the doctor sewed eighteen stitches into the skin of my inside right forearm, just above the wrist. I remember a policeman coming through the curtain and telling me that little girls needed not to scream quite so loudly and that everything would be okay. I remember being told that had the cut occurred just a millimeter in one direction or another, I would have lost the use of my right hand.

Today I still stare at the scar, crawling diagonally like a hairy albino caterpillar across my wrist, and remember.

Scars are like that. They tell stories that help us remember. Stories of wounds. Stories of failures. Stories of imperfection. Stories of things we need to integrate into our present, of past pain that shapes us and makes us who we are.

It's tempting to think that scars always tell stories that are finished, with a neat "THE END" scrawled across a final page. That the presence of a scar pronounces an injury "all better." Sometimes. After surgery a scar may remain, but truly the cancer, the appendix, the impacted tooth, the calcified bone spur, or whatever horribleness was wrought on the body is gone. We are, indeed, all better.

But often a scar tells the story of a wound still in the process of healing and offers a promise of being somewhat better in the here and now of our days on earth and of eventual, complete redemption in our hereafter. The jagged Harry Potter–style slash across the forehead of my niece who survived an unimaginable car accident reminds us all that she did *not* die, she is *not* paralyzed, she is *not* without a voice. Yes, she sustained a traumatic brain injury and will likely struggle to live exactly as before. But her scar (make that *scars*—there are many on her small frame) demonstrates that God was present with her in the accident, remains present in her recovery, and is redeeming that tragedy into a new offering.

And not all scars are external, visible to the outside world. Every one of us carries within certain scars on our souls. A wounding from a bully's name-calling. A horrific ripping from divorce. Death's cavernous hollow. Incest's shameful slash. Personal failures that pock our pasts.

Whether in process or marching toward full healing, whether within or without, a scar tells the story of a redeemed wound—a redemption that is both now and eventual. Our greatest challenge is to embrace the eventual in our now and live the truth of what *is* as well as what will more fully be one day.

As we consider the five places of beauty in our beings, the element of scar brings us to a beautiful integration of who we were, are, and will be. Can we see our painful stories—our scars—the way God sees them?

Let's look at different aspects, each erupting in a different format in our lives and leaving its own mark on our beings.

Blemish

I think the photo is from second grade. A white, stretchy hair band clamps my feathery, brown hair back from my face, while below my ears, exact curls kiss the sailor-style collar of my dress. I'm coyly looking at the camera, head slightly cocked per the instructions of the photographer. "Now tilt your head a bit to the left—the left! That's it! Now look up! Say 'Cheese!'" I obey, tilting my head just slightly more. Click! I'm done and back at my student desk in minutes.

When the photos arrived a few weeks later, our class was giddy. I always loved the moment when the cellophane-windowed envelope with my name was presented and I peeked out at myself from within. Just a hint of "me." I turned the envelope over, opened the flap, and my face fell. Not the face in the picture—my actual face. Because there, staring back at me with sailor collar, hair band, and curls was a part of me I hadn't planned on being in the picture: the straight part of my hair in the back. The part that hadn't been curled. The part that hung limp and ugly. That last tilt of my head had revealed what I had hoped to hide:

my hair had been curled only in the front and not in the back, because supposedly only the front would show in the picture.

That second grade photo taught me a lesson about school pictures for sure: curl *all* hair, front and back, because you just never know. That snapshot also taught me a lesson about how the smallest blemish can burst my confidence in who I am and what I offer in my world.

Blemishes are imperfections. Sometimes we're born with them, like the wine-colored smear across my daughter's décolletage. Sometimes they erupt after an illness, leaving a reminder of its attack, like the chicken pox crater in my midforehead. Sometimes they announce a preventative treatment, like the tuberculosis poke on my arm. And sometimes blemishes erupt under a nostril or near an eyebrow or race across a cheek due to the everyday normal hormones of life when you're fifteen—and then still at fifty-five.

We tend to use the mirror as a faultfinder, pausing with sincere searching every chance we get. But honestly, blemishes are not worth the investment of our worry. Blemishes can't hurt us once we learn to see them for what they are. In fact, blemishes can reveal an unexpected beauty.

In 2009 I took a trip to Kenya with the ONE Campaign. As an advocacy organization designed to eradicate extreme poverty and disease, ONE.org centers its attention on the health of Africa's poorest. Ten mom bloggers were invited to view the on-the-ground efforts of global aid in agriculture, microenterprise, maternal health, education, and the end of HIV/AIDS. I was included in the ten, and my life was imprinted with lasting dents by my fellow mom bloggers.

Among them was Karen Walrond, lawyer, engineer, photographer, TED talk presenter, wife, mom, and blogger of Chookooloonks.com. (*Go look* at her work! Wow!) In case you're curious, she picked the name *chookooloonks* for her site because it's a word from her native country of Trinidad. A term of endearment, used especially for children, it means something like English's equivalent of "darling" or "sweetheart."

What grabbed me most about Karen was her view of beauty. Karen is convinced we are all—every one of us—*uncommonly beautiful*. And in fact, in her book *The Beauty of Different*, Karen shared her personal belief that the very thing that makes us different makes us beautiful.[2] In her TED talk she said, "I believe the thing about us that might be a little weird . . . that other kids made fun of us when we were little kids, is the source of our beauty."[3]

Karen's trick to seeing the beauty of different is to apply a principle of photography: "Look for the light."[4] Watch for it. Study it. Embrace it when you see it.

Some differences slice more stunning scars that last well beyond the elementary years. Seeing the beauty of different in such imperfections is challenging but possible. Take Camryn Berry. A rare disease, fibrous dysplasia, caused a baseball-sized tumor to form in her left cheek. Kids were cruel, and fourteen-year-old Camryn was bullied behind her back and before her face. While she struggled as a child, she eventually grew to see the beauty in her differentness. Unexpectedly, a friend came to warn her of the bullying and provided protection. Later the deformity decreased the sight in her left eye to the point where she could hardly see at all. Her response? Camryn peered deeper and began to notice a certain beauty in her hazy, blurry, new-normal world. "It's like having a different lens on your Canon [camera]. It opens a whole new world of opportunity. Why would I want to give that up all to see the world like everybody else sees it?"[5]

Uncurled hair or customized coiffure. Gap-toothed or orthodontia-formed smile. Quiet or quirky. Smooth-talker or stutterer. Look in the mirror, find your imperfection, your blemish, your *different*, and discover its beauty.

Back to my second-grade school photo. Truly, if I view it in such a way, I see a picture of a little girl grieving the breakage of her divorced parents, who wanted so very much to be thought of as "cute"—at least on the outside. She sat while her mom made time to brush and fix her hair, the best she could before heading to her big-city job. On command, the little girl turned her head "just so" and smiled for the camera. And the camera obediently caught her differentness. I look for her light, and I see. There: I see beauty.

Wound

Certain life-altering scar sources lie deep in our beings. These painful injuries—not surface blemishes of differences or health issues—require careful and compassionate consideration. A few years back I wrote a whole book on this topic—my personal scar story.[6]

The wounds of my first and second families sliced me through, leaving scars that today tell stories of who I am, what I've learned, how I see God and his love, and how I live differently on the other side of broken, where there's beauty. I embrace the hope of Victor Frankl's observation, "In some way, suffering ceases to be suffering at the moment it finds a meaning."[7]

I'm not telling you anything you don't know here. You're well acquainted with the grief of being wounded. Pretty much every single time before I speak on *The Beauty of Broken*, I'm thinking I'm the only one. I find out afterward, in the bustle of people gathering their purses and shuffling their bulletins, that I'm not. Women and men alike, teens and elders, *everybody* is broken. We just think we're the only ones. *Hissssss!* Because of our brokenness, and our view of it as disqualifying us from contributing to life around us, we struggle to see any good—*beauty*—in our painful scar stories.

We have work to do here to discover that God brings beauty in the broken. The "hard" of the matter is that wounds that come from the hands of another leave dramatic scars that tell formative stories. God gets this.

There's yet another injury that occurs when we slip in our humanity and make a mess ourselves: failure. Failure leaves a scar of shame that threatens to define our days forever. God gets this too. He scarred his Son with nails to free us from living under such a hissing curse of shame.

In the latter years of my second family's breaking, God began to show me that while there surely were wounds coming at me from the hands of others, I was inflicting wounds as well, some on myself and many on others.

Down I went into the necessary humiliation of pride recognition. I truly thought that if I did everything right as a woman,

wife, mother, and leader, then I'd achieve the formulaically perfect results of a happy marriage, perfect family with perfect kids,
and a shiny, bright ministry. It took breakage to see my arro-
gance and my resulting judgment of others. (*Their kids were so
rebellious because they're never home with them! Their marriage
broke up because she let herself go!* You know the drill.) The thing
is, there's no formula for perfect. God isn't interested in us being
perfect anyway. He's more into reality and the redemption he
died to provide. Redemption comes only when we recognize our
need for it by falling down.

But oh, how scraped up we get falling down! Scars cover our
knees, from the falling and from the getting back up and realizing we have to go back down in prayer for forgiveness. Even after
we've crawled in confession to God and, at his directive, to those
we've wronged, we still struggle. The hardest person to forgive
is yourself.

I had known my neighbor, Nancy, pretty much ever since we
moved into the small subdivision where her husband unofficially
served as mayor. But I didn't know her well, nor had I heard the
personal scar story she kept concealed in the basement of her
being.

She came to our biweekly Bible study quietly but with an
eager anticipation. As we turned the pages of the book of John
and encountered various examples of Jesus changing lives,
Nancy's story emerged bit by bit. Her childhood faith. Her early
married days. Her current need in her late sixties to come back
to God. And then, her secret scar story: a horrible day when, as a
young mom, she allowed her early-elementary-school-age child

to go to a nearby park with a friend and without her or another adult. Nancy had given her little boy a specific time to return and warned him to stay away from the muddy pond in the park. Their family had an event later in the afternoon. He wasn't to get dirty.

The next thing Nancy heard was the doorbell. Her son and his friend had engaged in a competition: who would win in the race to the pond. But instead of stopping at the edge, her son plunged into the pond. A stranger walking by was hailed to help and heroically dragged the flatlined body from the muck. For days Nancy and her husband didn't know if their son would survive. He did—with a brain injury—and forty-some years later, Nancy watches him struggle to find work and to make an independent life.

"I'll never forgive myself," Nancy said.

The words sat heavily in the room of neighbors. One woman said, "But isn't that the point of grace? We mess up, but God still forgives. Right?"

It hit us all that maybe the way Nancy could best help her son today would be to forgive herself for her long-ago choice.

Nancy bowed her head and received a prayer that folded like a bandage over her whole heart, then offered words of her own in response. When she looked up through her tears, her face shone with relief and gratitude. I thought about a line I'd read in an article: "If we keep our stories to ourselves, they die there."[8] Part of us dies as well. But when we see and share our stories, admitting our neediness, God's redemption slips over our pain and begins the healing we so desperately need.

Scars tell stories of pain—and redemption. Our brokenness provides a pedestal for the display of God's beauty. As Paul wrote in 2 Corinthians 4:7, "We have this treasure in jars of clay to show that this all-surpassing power is from God and not from us." When we see our scars the way God sees them, we see beauty in our broken.

One autumn afternoon while on a trip in a small village in England, I stopped in an antique shop for a tiny excursion. In the back, stacked in a heap, I discovered a set of six antique china plates. They caught my attention because they looked so similar to the plates from my grandmother's plate collection—my most precious legacy from her—that had been displayed on a three-shelf hutch on my dining room wall. In the very season in which everything seemed to be falling off of the walls in my life, some-how that hutch had lost its grip on the wall and fell, smashing every single plate to smithereens. The sound haunts me still.

I picked up the stack and began to thumb through the plates. Suddenly I stopped. The second plate was cracked straight through and yet held together in sturdiness. Curious, I turned it over. On the back of the plate, like railroad tracks along the crack, metal staples had been inserted. What? Back and forth, I turned the plate over in wonder. Going through the rest of the stack, I discovered several others were similarly repaired. A tag taped on the top plate read "Victorian Era."

Ever so carefully, I carried the stacked treasure find up to the proprietress and asked, "Can you tell me about these plates and the staples?"

"Oh sure—they're from the Victorian era. That was a method of china repair employed then. They used brass and metal rivets, or staples like these." She pointed to the back of the plate.

"Why would anyone bother?" I wondered aloud.

"Well, if you had a choice to eat off of a wooden board or a repaired piece of porcelain china, what would you do?"

Indeed, I thought, *how true.* But that's what God does, isn't it? He doesn't throw us away when we break. He repairs. He redeems. God "stapled" his own Son to the cross that we might have a shot at hope. The stapled line of a scar tells the story of his love in our lives.

I have to think that scars and their stories are important to God. Really important. For when Jesus appeared to the disciples after his death, he brought his scars for show-and-tell. John reported Thomas wanting to see "the nail marks in his [Jesus'] hands" in John 20:25, and Jesus inviting Thomas, "Put your finger here; see my hands. Reach out your hand and put it into my side" (John 20:27). Jesus' scars were the real deal. The Greek word for hand really included both the wrist and the forearm.[9] Jesus had hung from the cross, fastened with metal spikes through his wrists and his feet. In order to demonstrate he was the same Jesus, he rose from the dead with the scars of his suffering still visible.

Scars proved Jesus to be the Savior. The scars of Jesus tell the story of our salvation.

Sarah Young wrote (in God's voice), "I am a God who heals. I heal broken bodies, broken minds, broken hearts, broken lives, and broken relationships." Yet in this very same entry she wrote of God, "I rarely heal all the brokenness in a person's life."[10] We wonder why, don't we? Why doesn't God heal *all* our brokenness? Why does he leave us with scars?

There's a little-known story in 2 Samuel 9 that I've grown to love over the years. David had become king, and in an effort to keep his promise to Jonathan to always show kindness to Jonathan's household (1 Samuel 20:15), he asked if there were any relatives remaining. A servant named Ziba from the household of Saul (Jonathan's father and the first king of Israel) reported that Jonathan had a son who was lame in both feet. That's how he described the son: "lame in both feet." Not how old he was or his profession or how many children he had. Nope; just, "There is still a son of Jonathan; he is lame in both feet" (2 Samuel 9:3). The son's name was Mephibosheth. In 2 Samuel 4:4 we learn that earlier in Mephibosheth's life, when he was only five years old, Jonathan and Saul were killed in the battle on Mount Gilboa. When news reached Jezreel, where Mephibosheth lived, his nurse picked him up to flee. But she tripped and fell, and both of Mephibosheth's ankles were broken, leaving him lame for life.

Now a grown man, Mephibosheth was summoned before King David, and David kept his long-pledged promise to his dear friend Jonathan, restoring land and position to Mephibosheth.

The story ends with this line in 2 Samuel 9:13: "And Mephibosheth lived in Jerusalem, because he always ate at the king's table; he was lame in both feet."

We meet Mephibosheth as a lame man and we leave him as a lame man. His scars remain. What is changed by the grace of the king of Israel is that Mephibosheth is treated as the king's very son. Our relationship of redemption in God's kingdom is current and real-time, but the healing from this world's infirmities may not find completion until we leave it.

We tend to think we have to be "done" in order to share the stories of our scars. Tied up with a bow. Pretty—or at least prettier. Not true. Just as Jesus returned with his scars intact in order to glorify the God who raised him (treasure in a jar of clay!), we honor God when we reveal the beauty in our broken.

But wait—doesn't it make more sense to keep the bandage on, allowing the wound to heal more before revealing it in story? Well, there is that. At times we just might need additional time and protection for more healing to happen. And so might other folks who have shared in the creation of our scar stories. But living a *lifetime* of self-protection won't grow us—or others. As one pastor suggests, "We aren't doing any good for God or for the world, or for the people we love, if we aren't taking risks that will certainly wound us."[11]

Steve Wiens marveled that all of us are both glorious and wrecked:

> We are glorious in part because though we are wrecked, we have survived, and here we are, sipping coffee on a Thursday morning. We have somehow made it through all the tragedies of our lives, and at some point today, we may even let out a guffaw of laughter so loud it rattles the teeth of the person sitting across from us. It is a bit unbelievable, if you think about it.[12]

There is beauty in our broken and painful stories. Seeing ourselves the way God sees us—through the cracks of our brokenness, our blemishes, our wounds—changes everything. Suddenly I'm not the only one, and neither are you! And somehow there's more to enjoy, more to celebrate, more to discover, and more to *offer* because of the true beauty of our scars.

Becoming Beauty Full You

1. Tell Your Story in Freedom

Do you know how to tell your scar story? Henri Nouwen was a man well acquainted with pain. Take in his wisdom, and consider just where you are in the process of understanding your painful story. Then ask God to help you take the next step toward freedom.

> There are two ways of telling your story. One is to tell it compulsively and urgently, to keep returning to it because you see your present suffering as the result of your past experiences. But there is another way. You can tell your story from the place where it no longer dominates you. You can speak about it with a certain distance and see it as the way to your present freedom. The compulsion to tell your story is gone. From the perspective of the life you now live and the distance you now have, your past does not loom over you. It has lost its weight and can be remembered as God's way of making you more compassionate and understanding toward others.[13]

2. Scart Project

How can you turn your scar story into art (scart!)? Create a mosaic made from shards of broken pottery, a mixed-media painting, or jewelry made from pieces of your past.

For example, select a china plate (a salad plate is best). On the back, write several words that express your personal scar story. Place the plate in a gallon-size plastic bag and zip it closed. Then take a hammer and hit the plate with one sharp blow. Jagged pieces should result. Hit it again if you prefer smaller pieces.

Then select a shard of your choice, sand the edges (careful now!), glue on a jewelry clasp, and string some cord to create a necklace. Voilà! You can wear your scart project as a symbol of your story!

3. God Uses the Broken

Do you believe God can use your brokenness for his purposes? Consider the many scriptural examples:

- God used two broken stone tablets to cause the Israelites to repent of their disobedience.
- God used broken earthen vessels (pitchers that covered torches) to give the impression of an enormous army accompanying Gideon and to cause his enemies to pull back in dread.
- God used a broken heart to return King David to himself.
- God used a broken roof to provide access for a cripple to be lowered by four faithful friends into the healing presence of Jesus.
- God used broken loaves to feed five thousand and then some.
- God used broken fishing nets to challenge the disciples to depend on him rather than on their own

efforts for their needs.

- God used a broken flask of nard to express the love that flows out of a relationship with him.
- God used a broken ship to steer Paul to the island of Malta to reveal the gospel to the natives there.
- God used a broken body, pierced for our sins, to provide salvation for all humankind.[14]

nine

SWAY

Beauty in Your Influential Legacy

My world is filled with beautiful things; they are meant to be pointers to Me, reminders of My abiding Presence.

—Sarah Young[1]

I dragged empty cardboard boxes—the kind used for shipping fruit to grocery stores—into my garage and turned them upside down. Carefully, I created neat rows and positioned at each cardboard "desk" some sort of child-sized seat: a carpet square, a toddler chair left over from my earlier years, a stool. Once I had things arranged, I, the teacher, walked between the rows of desks, teaching my imaginary students. I was eight years old.

At Christmastime that year, I asked for a blackboard. A giant, official schoolteacher, free-standing chalkboard. Santa delivered it to my garage, and I spent hours scrawling across it in pink, blue, and yellow chalk. With much determination, I coaxed several neighborhood preschoolers and kindergarten-ers into my after-school classroom. They sat, raptly listening, while I read from *The Little Engine That Could* and neatly printed questions about the story across my chalkboard. One weeknight I invited their parents to munch brownies, sign their names in my little guestbook, and view their children's drawings that I'd thumbtacked to the exposed studs in my garage walls. (Can you believe these parents actually showed up and participated? I can't imagine how my mother explained her daughter to them!)

Looking back, I realize it wasn't the kids and their attention I was after. I didn't really like little children all that much. I was discovering my sway.

Sway. Influence. From the innermost concentric circles of our lives, as we care for pets, hold babies, manage homes, drive carpools, gather girlfriends, teach classes, volunteer for field days, run departments, and cast our votes, we women naturally and intrinsically influence. We sway.

The evangelical universe seems a bit squeamish about the topics of women and influence twined together in the same sentence. Throats lump, palms sweat, and everyone checks their phones. Not gonna go there.

You might assume such hesitations come from men. Not always. In my experience women also bump on the concept of seeing themselves as people with sway.

In both the church and the parachurch, in both blue-collar and professional workplaces, Woman peers at the platform, down the halls, over cubicle walls, and around the shaping of the mission and work, and she sees very little in the way of female role models. She scours the perimeters for an entrance into circles of influence and finds doors shut, locked, and sometimes even double-bolted. Edging back from the lack of examples, Woman concludes what she has feared: she does not, after all, possess influence. No woman does. Surely, if she did, God would have opened a door and brought her through.

I like the way Parker J. Palmer lifted my gaze to see the topic of influence—and leadership—as a natural expression of every human's offering, given by God to us all.

> "Leadership" is a concept we often resist. It seems immodest, even self-aggrandizing, to think of ourselves as leaders. But if it is true that we are made for community, then leadership is everyone's vocation, and it can be an evasion to insist that it is not. When we live in the close-knit ecosystem called community, everyone follows and everyone leads. . . .
>
> I lead by word and deed *simply because I am here doing what I do.* If you are also here, doing what you do, then you also exercise leadership of some sort.[2]

Add to Palmer's perspective that of Judith Couchman, and we get a recipe for everyday sway that just might work for us as women: "Influence isn't about power and getting what we want. It's about servanthood and giving our best to others, whatever our position in life."[3]

So why don't we sway—or if we do, why don't we sway *more,* with greater confidence and commitment? God loves us! Why do we struggle so to see ourselves as he sees us, as women with *beauty full* sway?

Sway Struggles

The parking lot across from the television station was nearly empty at the early hour I arrived for the interview. I was a bit nervous being downtown, heading to a place I had never been before. I slid my car into a slot and walked across the street to the studio.

A few hours later I returned to the lot to discover a car parked directly behind mine, blocking my exit. What? I searched for the building that went with the lot and headed up its steps. Inside, I asked the receptionist about the matter.

Her eyebrows shot up. "Oh! You parked in Mr. Brown's spot!"

Okaaaay, I thought. "Can you please ask Mr. Brown to move his car so I can leave?"

"Oh, you'll have to ask him. He's very strict about these things. Let me buzz him." The receptionist shakily put down the receiver and directed me down the hall to Mr. Brown's office.

He looked up as I entered, a wizened little man with gray caterpillar brows crawling above his intense gaze. Kinda scary.

"Excuse me, Mr. Brown. It seems that your car is blocking mine in the lot, and I need to leave."

"You bet it is!" he bellowed at me. "You parked in my spot! You can just wait until I go to court at 11:00!"

"Oh, I am so sorry, Mr. Brown. I didn't know it was your spot. Could I get you to move your car now? I have some meetings—"

"Well, you should have known better, and you can just wait. Now get out of my office!"

My legs rattled as I clicked into obedience and practically ran down the hall to the reception area, where I perched in a chair and peered at the clock. It was 8:30 a.m. Mr. Brown was asking me to sit here and wait for two and a half hours? I had meetings! I had commitments to keep! My staff was expecting me back at the office! And yet there I sat, paralyzed.

Sympathetically, the receptionist offered me coffee. "He's like that," she conceded.

Thirty minutes went by, and I sat and stewed. Who did he think he was? I scoured mental files for arguments I could pose to get myself free. Each fell flat as I played it out in my imagination. My palms sweated. My mouth dried out. I had to pee. Finally, I gathered my courage and asked the receptionist to buzz him again to find out if he would see me once more. She did, and he agreed.

I stood before his desk like a schoolgirl before the principal. "Mr. Brown, I'm wondering what you are needing from me. I have apologized for my error. I am truly sorry. Please, sir, I need to ask you again to move your car."

He grimaced and continued working, harrumphing under his breath. "No way."

"All right then. If you will not move your car, I will be forced to call the police and let them know that you are holding me in your office against my will."

Mr. Brown looked up, met my stare—and smiled. A twinkle appeared in his hooded eyes. "Well, there you go!" He rose from his desk, flourished his arms toward the door, grabbed his car keys, and guided me out to the parking lot. In minutes, I was gone.

With Mr. Brown, my *sway* was necessary to move him from his agenda to mine. If I wouldn't stand up for myself, he sure wasn't going to make my day easy.

We women are afraid to use our sway. In her bestselling book, *Lean In*, Sheryl Sandberg commented,

> Fear is at the root of so many of the barriers that women face. Fear of not being liked. Fear of making the wrong choice. Fear of drawing negative attention. Fear of overreaching. Fear of being judged. Fear of failure. And the holy trinity of fear: the fear of being a bad mother/wife/daughter.[4]

As in my experience with Mr. Brown, we women struggle with certain fears regarding our sway. Perhaps most obvious is the struggle we face with *gender*. We doubt women are influential; therefore, we shouldn't lead. Mr. Brown was a man, and I instinctively obeyed him. We also face a struggle of *season*. We are either young and haven't fully owned our influence, or we're old(er) and distrust our relevance and value (even though we *know* we're wise!). Mr. Brown was *way* older than me, and I was intimidated by his bullying. And we face a struggle of *adequacy*. We doubt our abilities. We aren't smart enough, trained enough, experienced enough, confident enough. Mr. Brown was a lawyer, and I didn't think I had the skills to present my case adequately to him.

Can I just say it? Our sway struggles are—again—the result of the Hiss.

Gender Sway

In seminary I spent months teasing apart some of the most complicated passages regarding "the role of women:" Genesis 1–3, 1 Corinthians 11, 1 Timothy 2–3, 1 Peter 3. Scripture seemed to clearly state that men and women were created equally and both in the image of God. It became clear that women were free and gifted to lead in any capacity in the workplace and in the parachurch. The one nut I couldn't crack was that of senior authority—pastoral authority—in the church. To be honest, I could agree with brilliant commentators on both sides—the complementarians who held that gifts were gender-based, and the egalitarians who believed gifts were given equally to both genders. But in that era, I leaned into and landed on the position that a woman couldn't serve as senior pastor in the local church. To me it seemed *safer* to allow that only a male could serve as senior pastor, holding the highest level of authority in the church. I didn't want to mess up in such a matter. With great sincerity, I chose *safe* in order to honor God and stay on the side of obedience.

In my earliest professional days, serving as dean of women at a Bible college, I accepted the school's parameter that I could counsel both men and women, and I could teach both men and women on secular topics like psychology and counseling. But I could not teach men on ministry and Bible topics, and I could only "share" in chapel and not preach. Though my theological convictions embraced the freedom for women to do more than this, and while the college was not a church but rather an institution, I yielded my sway to the standards of the school.

While teaching a course on women in ministry—to women only—I was stunned at the resistance within my female students to investing their gifts. While most professed dreams of marriage and children, they skittered away from other shores of influence, leadership, *sway.* What could a woman do? What *should* a woman do? Didn't they realize that only a fourth to a third of their lives would actually be spent in the season of raising children? Sure, the remaining three-fourths would involve some forever-mothering and then possibly the totally rewarding investment of grandmothering, but what would they do with the rest of their sway? Together we stepping-stoned across scriptures and spiritual gifts and natural talents to discover some meaningful places of investment in addition to the home.

Years later I led women who did see themselves as leaders. Some thirty thousand moms annually (cumulatively nearly a million moms over the decades) waded into the influence of volunteer leadership at MOPS International. Add to that millions of moms who would be moved to embrace their own leadership sway by this wave of volunteers. I unapologetically led our team to lead leaders to lead others. Today these leaders continue to produce women who widely invest their sway in the workplace, the church, and the parachurch.

Somewhere in the last decade or so, I began to feel a personal nudge at my "safe" position on the role of women. Something just didn't sit right with it anymore. It's not that I had felt called to perform outside the parameters I'd adopted. For years I sat under the authority of my male senior pastor, but at his request, I happily accepted invitations to preach in our church. I traveled and filled pulpits in other churches at their pastors' requests. I performed funerals and weddings. Outside the church, I led a parachurch organization with men and women on the staff and board. I served on other boards. All these platforms fit the boundaries of the biblical conclusions I'd drawn.

While my parameters weren't limiting me, an unrest rose up from what I felt as a kind of dishonesty brewing within. While I'd sided with one brilliantly articulated and well-respected position on the role of women, I knew the other side was worthy of consideration as well. Gradually I realized that I'd chosen my stance not so much out of hermeneutical weight but out of a desire to "choose the lesser evil." Fear had been my main motivation. I felt convicted to pause. To reevaluate both my conclusion and the motivation behind it.

I ordered and listened to a ninety-minute study from Willow Creek Church by John Ortberg as he led a class through every passage that touched on the role and gifting of women in Scripture. In one spot, I stopped, backed up, and replayed his words over and over and over:

> Now, here's the particular point I want to make here: This is important because people sometimes speak as if the position that honors biblical authority is to say, "We'll remain hierarchical [complementarian]; we'll restrict women's practice of their gifts, unless you can remove every reservation from every difficult passage. Unless every reservation is removed, we'll stay hierarchical. And I just want to point out that for any given complex issue, that's not a correct hermeneutic. It

dishonors the notion of authority of the whole of Scripture. The right interpretive approach is to say, "I will go with the preponderance of evidence of Scripture on a complex issue."[5]

That got my attention.

I restudied the commentaries. I picked up Scot McKnight's *The Blue Parakeet* and Christian Smith's *The Bible Made Impossible* and reevaluated my hermeneutics. I could still see both sides of the argument. And I could see that living my life trying to be "safe" was no way to honor God. Out of a passion to allow the freedom God well may allow, I widened my personal view of parameters of how a woman can use her gifts—*even* in the church. My understanding now is that women can preach, women can pastor, women can serve. All roles are open to women, and no male authority is necessary to "cover" a woman's offering.

It's not just in the arena of the church that we women wrestle with gender-based fear of sway. When the old lawyer blocked my exit, I gave way to fear. He was a man. I was a woman. I submitted to his authority. Period. Such an idea is planted in us as tiny girls, isn't it? The lower timbre of a male voice, the sandpaper cheek of our fathers, the sheer strength of a man's physique—all are so *different* and *powerful*.

As we mature, we women assess our options: home and family *or* career. Since most of us want home and family, we rank career second—and for good reasons—for many years. A 2012 McKinsey survey of more than four thousand employees of leading companies found that 36 percent of men wanted to reach the corner suite, compared to only 18 percent of women.[6] While surely many based their choice on family, there may be something else going on here—more fear. Lois Frankel attributed this statistic partly to women's reticence to take the lead; when they do exhibit leadership behaviors, they receive a wide array of negative reactions from men *and* women, such as being called names, having their ideas challenged rather than built on, and being excluded from future meetings. She concluded, "Nice girls don't lead."[7]

Do you struggle with seeing how your gender has sway? Do you fear your own innate influence because you are a woman and women shouldn't lead?

Then consider this:

Influence is intrinsic to every human being. Male and female. Our actions affect others, for good or for evil, every day, from feeding a baby to emptying the garbage to carpooling to sitting at a boardroom table to preaching in the pulpit. Women (and men) are people of influence, and we cannot *not* exercise an effect on others through our efforts. Imagine the proverbial pebble in the pond here, or the butterfly effect. Because you and I are *here*, breathing and being, we are influencing others in our world.

Women, uniquely, have sway. From the curve of our bodies to the automatic rhythmic movement we adopt when we pick up a baby (even if the baby isn't our own), women were made to sway in a way that men were not: from the hip. With our influence and power, we women lead our babies to nurse, our toddlers to toddle, our pets to potty, our sisters and brothers to the family table, our parents toward assistance, our spouses toward connection, our friends toward growth, and our coworkers toward goals. We control the majority of household spending decisions, and we are raising the next generation. Today women are the world's single most powerful demographic.

God intends for women to invest our sway in his kingdom purposes. God made us in his image: male *and* female. It will take both men and women, fully committed to living out our influence, to accomplish God's kingdom purposes on this planet.

"The harvest is plentiful but the workers are few," Jesus said in Matthew 9:37. And then he instructed his disciples, "Ask the Lord of the harvest, therefore, to send out workers into his harvest field" (v. 38). Seems to me there just might be enough workers if more women were included in the pool of talent.

Whatever your position on the role of women, there is too much to be done to leave women out of the doing. God has created each and all of us to accomplish his purposes in this world, and he openhandedly extends to each of us an invitation to involvement. Be clear that this opportunity is not for women to the exclusion of men but rather for both men and women for the inclusion of us all.

Look at what was happening with women early on in Jesus' ministry in Luke 8:1–3, after a woman anointed Jesus at the home of Simon, the Pharisee:

> Jesus traveled about from one town and village to another, proclaiming the good news of the kingdom of God. The Twelve were with him, and also some women who had been cured of evil spirits and diseases: Mary (called Magdalene)

from whom seven demons had come out; Joanna the wife of Chuza, the manager of Herod's household; Susanna; and many others. These women were helping to support them out of their own means.

While the twelve disciples were decidedly male, they were not the only disciples. Jesus modeled the necessity of both genders in the fulfillment of his purposes. Further, his inclusion of women in his teaching, in his traveling, in his support, and in his ministry was radical for his day. It's still radical today.

Shauna Niequist, the daughter of Willow Creek Community Church's founders Bill and Lynne Hybels, spoke at a Q Conference on "What My Mother Taught Me." Concluding, she remarked, "Everyone benefits when women tap into the passions and use the gifts that God has given them. The church benefits. Families benefit. Marriages benefit. Businesses and nonprofits benefit. Everyone wins when women discover and live out of the gifts and the passions that God gave them."[8]

The sway struggle of gender gives way when we embrace the reality that God created women with influence—just as he did men—and that he intends for women to invest their influence to accomplish his kingdom purposes. God loves us and sees us as *beauty full* beings who possess *beauty full* sway.

Seasonal Sway

The investment of our influence, both personal and professional, alters as we age. My personal sway began in the years when I cared for my younger brother, wrestled codependently with my mother, interacted with friends in adolescence as I discerned "me" from "them," met and married my husband, raised my children, and buried my parents. It continues today as I parent adult children and grandparent their babies, as I live out my marriage and reach out in my neighborhood.

Professionally, my sway swung through my Young Life testimony utterances to serving the elderly in a retirement village while in seminary, to teaching at a Bible college, to leading a neighborhood Bible study and serving as CEO of MOPS International. These days I have my sway as I write and speak, cohost a national radio program, serve on boards, and mentor. My professional sway has ebbed and flowed.

In each season, I've seen my personal sway impact my professional, and vice versa. How true it is that *we* are God's workmanship. God is just as concerned with what is being formed *in* us as he is with what is being accomplished *through* us.

Each season layers our offerings into more rather than less. In our younger years, lack of age holds us back as we fear we don't know enough to meaningfully contribute. We gobble up the aging process, satiated by the sufficiency that each decade seems to serve us. Sixteen brings the independence of wheels. Turning twenty-one makes us "legal." Thirty brings legitimacy.

And then the whole aging thing goes a little wonky on us, each decade threatening diminishment. Forty brings ambivalence. We like who we are and what's behind and ahead, yet we begin to notice certain ebbings. Fifty surprises us with its sudden appearance. And sixty? Seventy? How did we get here?

Our culture reflects age back to us oh-so-negatively, branding our competencies as diminishing, our value as bygone. Not so. In reality, what happens is that our offerings mutate and change hues. Anne Lamott described, "I awoke this morning to find that the leaves in my heart have started changing color, from green to yellow, persimmon, and red."[9] My dear friend Carol was diagnosed with stage four ovarian cancer at age sixty. Stunned by this development in what others claim to be the most productive decade of life, she fought hard for health and was gracefully granted nearly a decade of remission. Today she invests meaningfully in the lives of her children and grandchildren, her husband and her church, several mentees and friends. She embraces her new, smaller world.

While our culture bucks the value of aging, we who round the corner of middle age grasp that the older we are, the more we understand who we are and just what we can contribute.[10] Rather than confining us, maturity expands us and our offerings. As Kelly Corrigan wrote in *The Middle Place,* "And just like every other person who has buried his childhood, I grow up."[11]

We move through the seasonal sway struggle when we embrace the idea that God's work in us in every stage prepares us for the next.

Adequate Sway

A deeply challenging sway struggle—one I still swing at and miss—is the struggle of *adequacy.* We doubt our abilities. We fear we aren't smart enough, trained enough, experienced enough, confident enough. We fear we aren't influential enough and that our leadership won't make any difference.

In her book *Dare Mighty Things,* Halee Gray Scott shared her research that revealed, "The myth that *no* Christian women can lead has given way to the myth that only exceptional or extraordinary women can lead."[12] We somehow excuse the exceptional as "having" to lead because they're so special and let ourselves off the hook because we conclude we are not.

She went on:

> We say that Mozart was an exceptional composer and that Ernest Hemingway was an exceptional author, but that Jane Austen was an exceptional *female* author and that Margaret Thatcher was an exceptional *female* prime minister. When it comes to women, our exceptionality is often associated with our gender, not our gifts. . . . It is almost as if we are surprised when a woman's gifting falls outside of traditionally accepted roles.[13]

Lois Frankel poked at our objections of inadequacy in her book *See Jane Lead.* In fact, she suggested that women are uniquely qualified to invest their influence because they *are* women. Women leaders are making great contributions to the companies in the for-profit and social sectors because they are more consultative, more collaborative, better at multitasking, more big-picture oriented, and more relationally driven while being fact oriented.[14]

Scripture is chock-full of women who invested their influence—swaying their way for God's kingdom purposes. In three of the four Gospels, Mary of Bethany anointed Jesus' body *before* his burial, in a moment when he could receive her gesture as the love offering it was meant to be. Before a room filled with religious leaders and the disciples as well, Mary testified through her action that she believed Jesus was the Messiah and challenged everyone present to decide who they believed he was.

As a result, Mary was ridiculed by the diners but honored by Jesus.

> "Why are you bothering her? She has done a beautiful thing to me. . . . *She did what she could.* She poured perfume on my body beforehand to prepare for my burial. Truly I tell you, wherever the gospel is preached throughout the world, what she has done will also be told, in memory of her." (Mark 14:6– 9, emphasis added)

Those five words of Jesus have freed me from the adequacy-based fear of investing who I am in influencing others. She did *what* she could.[15] Jesus honored Mary of Bethany not because she did *all* she could. Not because she did things *better* or more *exceptionally* than others. Jesus' words are that she did *what* she could. She brought a timely action in a moment when it could never be repeated and anointed Jesus' body before he died. Mary knew Jesus loved her, and she loved him back by living loved and investing who she was with her *beauty full* sway.

Swaying Together

God calls women to invest our influential legacy as women, who are adequate, in each season. But here's the thing: sway isn't only about you and me. Sway is also about *us*: women together. As we discover our sway, God will use us to woo other women to discover and invest as well.

I was one of six women in my seminary program. Even nearly forty years ago, God was clear to me about his responsibility and mine: *My job is to open the door. Yours is to go through it and, once on the other side, to put your foot in the doorway to hold it open for the next woman coming after you.*

Today that's my job description and calling: go through each door God opens and keep my foot in the doorway for the next woman, in all kinds of areas and on all kinds of subjects. Like helping every woman everywhere understand that God loves her and sees her as *beauty full*.

Are you that woman? I'm betting you are.

Wherever you are on the pathway to leadership—whether you suspect you might have gifts that aren't being used or you know you have influence but need a push to live it out—there's a doorway in front of you. Every *one* of us has influence that God intends for us to invest for his kingdom purposes.

God is opening doors for women everywhere—you and me, our mothers and our daughters, our neighbors and coworkers and fellow pew-sitters—to invest who we are and how he has gifted us as women in the world around us in order to accomplish his desires. He is calling us to recognize, utilize, maximize, and mobilize all he has placed in us to take his purposes further and farther. Whatever you call it—leadership, influence, *sway!*—it's time to move through the open doors and prop them open for the next *beauty full* women coming behind us.

Becoming Beauty Full You

1. Discover the Parameters of Your Sway

Dr. Alice Matthews outlined the four basic positions on women's role in the church.[16] Take some time to study and discern which describes your understanding of what the Scriptures say. Give yourself permission to fully explore and even try on each position. Resist the temptation to let someone else (smarter, more biblically trained, more professional) make this decision for you. Pray for discernment and leading from God for your own personal position.

	EQUAL	SUBORDINATE
Can hold positions of authority	Women are equal with men and therefore should have positions of authority within the church.	Women are subordinate to men but can have positions of authority in the church.
Cannot hold positions of authority	Women are equal with men but should not have positions of authority within the church.	Women are subordinate to men and therefore should not have positions of authority in the church.

2. Understand Your Season of Sway

Dr. Deborah Newman suggested there are several seasons to a woman's development. The tasks of each season can affect how we both recognize and utilize our influence, and serve as a kind of timeline to assess our influential legacies. Pinpoint how your current age affects your sway. Challenge yourself to invest *all* your influence now while also looking to be fully present in the ages to come.

> *Ages 14–18—I must not be like my mother. . . .* An adolescent girl's major task is to develop a sense of identity apart from those of her parents. . . .
>
> *Ages 19–29—I have both male and female characteristics.* By this stage, a healthy woman has developed confidence in her sexual identity. . . . She observes both male and female characteristics in her personality and develops strengths in both areas. . . .
>
> *Ages 30–50—I am my mother.* During this stage of womanhood, we begin to understand our unique gifts and influences on the world . . . .
>
> For most of us the earliest memories we have of our mothers were when they were about these ages themselves. Their identity and ways of life subtly influenced us, even when we found ourselves separated from them by distance or death. . . .
>
> *Ages 50 and up—I am a woman.* A woman with a healthy feminine identity at this stage lives with confidence that she is deeply loved and deeply valuable to God and others.[17]

3. Strategize Your Sway

What can only you do? One way to strategize your sway is to honestly assess your unique offering of influence.

In your home, where can only you invest your influence?

In your place of work, where can only you invest your influence?

In your marriage, in your friendships, in your family of origin, in your church, where can only you invest your influence?

4. Strengthen Your Sway with Men

Desi McAdam works in the male-dominated tech industry. Consider her suggestions for holding your own—and then some.

- Read about the imposter syndrome.
- Don't send cues that minimize your talents. Don't apologize all the time or say things like, "I'm not good at this . . ."
- If you have male coworkers who tell inappropriate jokes, be direct and tell them to stop.
- Surround yourself with like-minded women you can be emotionally open with. Share your frustrations and successes, and go to them for advice.
- Recruit more women and help them become successful.
- Don't fear criticism.
- Recognize the differences between how men and women think and lead.

- Be aware of your own unconscious biases.
- Negotiate. Stand up for yourself and your responsibilities.[18]

5. Start Your Own Group of Professional Women Friends
Diane Paddison served as COO of Trammell Crow for decades. There she experienced firsthand the need for women friends. In her book *Work, Love, Pray*, she suggested steps to create support for yourself.

- Keep it simple. No agenda. No book to study. No pressure to maintain perfect attendance. And don't meet too often.
- Keep it relational. It's about "us." Our lives. The things that keep us up at night.
- Keep it small. Five or fewer is best.
- Keep it fluid. Don't think of your group as a permanent commitment. Give yourself permission to stop or take a break.
- Keep it confidential. Invite women with whom you've had some history and whom you know you can trust.
- Keep it within your generation. You will have many similar issues around which to connect and support each other due to the stage of life you are experiencing at the time.
- Keep it out of your company. You won't get bogged down in office issues and you'll be more likely to be completely honest with each other.[19]

part three

FULL

Living Your Beauty Full Life

Stuck at the end of a word, the suffix *-ful* means "full of" or "characterized by."

Most of us miss its offering. Tacked on to a rich concept comes an easy-to-overlook qualifier, like a store-bought cookie at the completion of a holiday feast. An unnecessary mouthful when we're already satiated.

"*Ful*?" Redundant. Repetitive. Superfluous. Unnecessary.

But wait. What if we look further? How does this little, tip-of-the-tail word wag our understanding of a concept's true meaning?

Wonder*ful* = full of wonder.

Merci*ful* = full of mercy.

Beauti*ful* = full of beauty.

Standing alone, separated out as a word all its own, *-ful* becomes *full* and offers an important connotation.

Full = Containing as much as possible, having no empty space; not lacking anything, complete.

To be full is to be complete, whole—though not necessarily finished. To live life to the *brim*—and *more*!

Beautiful = full of beauty.

Beauty Full = beauty to the brim—and more!

Hello, Beauty Full.

ten

TO THE BRIM— AND MORE!

They have decided they are beautiful, and because of that, everyone believes them.

—Mandy Arioto[1]

I get stuck. Right here—after *Hello, Beauty* and before *Full*— I stop.

Why not simply *Hello, Beauty*? Isn't that enough? After all, discovering that God sees me as his *beauty* is magnificent! Plenty! That God sees my voice, vessel, womb, scar, and sway as places of beauty—and that he wants me to see each the same way—wow. This is *huge*!

I'll stop here. Surely I don't deserve even this much, right? Why go all the way to *Hello, Beauty FULL*?

Where do you get stuck, dear beauty? Is there a spot where you brake your being, eager but fearful? Is there a "This is too good to be true" kind of thinking slamming through your soul? Do you share my stuttering hesitancy at the concept of *full*?

Two thousand years ago, Jesus sat by a well and waited. He was tired from traveling the distance from Judea to Galilee. Now partway there, in Samaria, the human God was thirsty, and he sat by the very well dug by his servant Jacob and passed down to Jacob's son, Joseph. It was noon, and the sun blazed down on his shoulders. Below, he could see the fresh water forming from the deep underground spring, but without a bucket or other device, look was all he could do. The one who formed the deep—the one who fairly sloshed with creative flow—sat by a well and thirsted.

At this unlikely hour, when no one left the shade of home for the scorch of heat, a woman approached. Countless commentators have cataloged her sins: too many men, not enough marriage, a heretical faith. Jesus asked her for a drink, and while she stumbled over the impossibility of his request—a Jew requesting a drink from an unclean foreigner—Jesus rearranged her world. She, too, was parched, though she had yet to realize the extent of her need. Nor the degree of the fullness Jesus was offering. Her heart and soul knew no understanding of the reality of how Jesus truly saw her: *beauty full*. Like us, had she grown so accustomed to "empty" that she expected nothing else?

"If you knew the gift of God and who it is that asks you for a drink, you would have asked him and he would have given you living water" (John 4:10).

Jesus spoke straight into her emptiness, his words echoing in her void. The woman objected. Surely he could not mean *her*?

"Everyone who drinks this water will be thirsty again, but whoever drinks the water I give them will never thirst. Indeed, the water I give them will become in them a spring of water welling up to eternal life" (John 4:13–14).

What? In the arid climate of Samaria, no more thirst? When that dry woman dragged her bucket forward, Jesus offered *living* water—not from a well but from himself. Actually, the sense here is not just a spring of water welling up but rather welling up and *over*.

God knows our needs. In Jesus, God himself thirsted. God understands our soulful dependence—so much that in Jesus, God came to fill us with an unending source of sustenance.

Perhaps the ultimate expression of God's desire to fill us comes in John 10:10, where Jesus invited, "I have come that they may have life, and have it to the full."

So why do we settle for empty?

We Expect Empty

The woman at the well came for a bucket of water to wash her robe, to mix with flour for her bread, to soothe her throat. Hers was a life of survival in which empty was her constant companion.

Men had come and gone, had taken what they wanted from her and left her empty. She went to the town well not in the cool hours of daybreak, as most respected women would do, arm in arm with their cul-de-sac buddies. No, she went in midday, when she could be certain she would be left alone. No jeering. No name-calling. No sideways glances.

In her emptiness, I see my own. Do you see yours? Our empty

buckets clank down on rock: Not enough kindness to offer in a busy early morning. Not enough money to make it through the month. Not enough patience to last until the homework is complete. Not enough love to stretch over a growing chasm in a friendship or a marriage.

Maybe you climbed out of poverty where you never felt full, or survived abuse that clawed out your heart, or latch-keyed life as a child left alone too much for too long. Maybe you're a mom surviving a long season of sleeplessness or a caregiver dispensing around-the-clock support to a loved one. Maybe you spill yourself out to serve the lives of those around you, your emptiness seemingly the natural result of being broken and spilled out for Jesus.

Empty can be a norm that we grow to endure and then expect.

My childhood well was a cavern of empty. A hollowed-out hunger that never seemed to get enough security, predictability, love. Today, as an adult in an unending relationship with God, how can I still feel empty? When Jesus lifts me, directing my lips to the pure drink of hope he offers, why do I continue to thirst? Is my struggle that I don't expect anything but empty, so I don't drink?

Yes. Another lie: *Hissssss*—empty is the way I'm *supposed* to be. Used up to the max so that no moment of life is wasted. Spent.

We Don't Understand Full

The woman at the well was filled with confusion. Stunningly, Jesus (a Jew) talked with her (a Samaritan woman; a woman from a different religion using a different set of scriptures and worshiping in a different place; a woman of questionable character) in broad daylight. She stood staring at Jesus, working to comprehend his words. The words, the setting, the Person—all were foreign to her world.

When it comes to *full*, we have some crazy understandings too. Our natural bent is toward scarcity—there's not enough to go around. Or as followers of Christ, we're not supposed to have what we want or as much as we want. Full seems gluttonous, even selfish. Full is for fancy folk like George Clooney and Kim Kardashian, not for everyday God-seekers like us.

We define *full* as "a sip." Even when we give way to an eruption of tears or a tirade of frustration or a pretzel of anxiety, and run like nightmare-tormented children to the lap of Jesus, we stay but a moment. We politely sip his presence, when our parched beings long to unendingly gulp open-mouthed. "There, there . . . ," we receive, only to jump up after ten seconds, swallowing sobs, fisting Kleenex, and returning to the flow, where it is so lovely to feel needed rather than needy.

That's enough, we tell ourselves. *Now get back to work. Now be quiet. Now step aside and let someone else have attention. You've had your turn. Make do with what you have.*

Like the Depression survivors who hoard string and plastic bags and rubber bands, we hold our one drop of full and try to make it last, oblivious to the ongoing and unending Source of filling—welling up and *over*—that is always at our disposal, that we were created to depend on, that we were created to enjoy!

In the days I struggled with seminary applications, I begged God to show me where to enroll, where to move, where to invest in training for his work. There was a school in a northern, cold, and somewhat scary-to-me city. It was well respected and offered the degree I wanted. And then there was a school in a gorgeous mountain community, tucked into a crevice between plains and mountains like a jewel cushioned in a ring box. It, too, offered the program I desired. Yet I struggled. I couldn't discern which to choose.

I met with a friend a year ahead of me in the process and asked his opinion. His answer was simply put: "Where do you *want* to go, Elisa?" Huh? My *wants* played into this decision? I poked about in my thinking and realized quickly that I *wanted* to go to Denver. My deep-in-the-heart-of-Texas being was surprisingly drawn to the geography and the beauty of Colorado.

"But shouldn't I pick the place where I will *suffer* more?" I asked my friend.

He laughed and responded, "Oh, you'll suffer for sure! No one escapes the preparation for ministry brought through suffering. But maybe God *wants* you to be where *you* want to be."

Why is it so hard for us to grasp that when Jesus says he came to give us life to the full, he means *full*? The word he uses means "rich and satisfying, extraordinary, profuse, copious, abundant, remarkable." Eugene Peterson put it this way in *The Message*: "I came so they can have real and eternal life, more and better life than they ever dreamed of" (John 10:10).

A life I actually *want* that includes having as much as I want. More than a sip. More than just *Hello, Beauty*. All the way to the brim of full.

We're Afraid of All That Full Might Include

The woman at the well recoiled against Jesus' intimate knowledge of all that filled her days and nights. Five husbands, and the one she was currently with wasn't even that. Full could have seemed incredibly dangerous to her. Besides, wouldn't her past prohibit her from such goodness?

If we're honest, we get nervous about God's desire to fill us. Full of what? Full from what? Frankly, at times we're disappointed by all that our supposedly good God has already allowed in our days. God's filling can include realities we don't want along with those we do.

I know. I've been emptied by life and its surprising potholes. A parent disappoints. A teen becomes pregnant. A loved one loses himself in addiction. A baby comes and goes with way too short of a life. Brokenness empties and empties and then empties some more.

Our buckets scrape on the dry rocks at the bottom of our wells. Where is the full—to the brim!—life Jesus promised? Right there in the empty. Because that's where Jesus is.

- God reveals his provision when we are neediest. "Blessed are the poor in spirit, for theirs is the kingdom of heaven" (Matthew 5:3).
- God reveals his beauty in our broken moments of life. "But we have this treasure in jars of clay to show that

this all-surpassing power is from God and not from us"
(2 Corinthians 4:7).

- God uses all things for our good. All means *all*. "And we
  know that in all things God works for the good of those
  who love him, who have been called according to his
  purpose" (Romans 8:28).

A full life includes the dark *and* the light. The trials *and*
the joys. The broken *and* the beautiful. The empty *and* the full.
Everything belongs.

My friend Kim shares that as she battled breast cancer,
God gently but clearly revealed to her some wonky beliefs that
were hanging her up. Kim and her husband are on staff with
an international ministry and carry the responsibility of raising financial support for their salaries. As she struggled with her
diagnosis, she realized she had slipped into an entitled way of
thinking: "Surely because I'm in God's work, I don't deserve cancer! Raising money for my salary is trial enough!"

As she fought, she saw how Jesus wanted to fill her mis-
thinking that led to emptiness with himself and his truth. She
also realized that while she wanted to protect her elementary-age
kids from seeing the awful in life, God was using her illness
to teach them about the body of Christ. "Just about the whole
church must have access to our garage keypad, as meals magi-
cally appeared in the cooler in our garage," she told me. Her kids
saw God use his people to respond to their family's needs.

Parker J. Palmer underlines how much fuller we actually
can be *because* of enduring the seasons of suffering: "Good

leadership comes from people who have penetrated their own inner darkness . . . and . . . who can lead the rest of us to a place of 'hidden wholeness' because they have been there and know the way."[2]

How do I miss full because it comes packaged differently than I expect? Opening to what God may allow in my life may open me to pain as well as pleasure, but he uses *all* to create fullness. Will we let him?

We Don't Understand How to Stay Filled

The woman at the well had given up on relationship. Every marriage she formed broke. She had been widowed, divorced, abandoned, ruined.

We, too, have been wounded. We've been left and abandoned. We've been overlooked and shunned. We get the empty of disappointing relationships.

And this is where Jesus comes offering a new way. "I have come that they may have life, and have it to the full," Jesus told his disciples in John 10:10. Lasting fullness that drenches our emptiness comes when we discover a relationship that doesn't run out. Seems simple, doesn't it? Trust Jesus. Let him love you. Right?

But there's more. Look at the sentence that comes just before this promise—right there, in the very same verse: "*The thief comes only to steal and kill and destroy*; I have come that they might have life, and have it to the full" (John 10:10, emphasis added).

Oh boy, oh boy, oh boy. I never noticed! There it is again: *Hissssss*. If we want life to the full, a life Jesus came to give, we surely need to let Jesus love us and fill us and change us—*and* we need to deal with the thief.

The hissssssssy thief. The one I overlook every day in my everyday. How is the thief still emptying the life Jesus came to give me to the full?

In some moments, I see the thief stealing my confidence, telling me I'm not enough and that I must replace myself with a more expert offering in order to have something to say. In the months of writing this book, I've wrestled to turn to other, seemingly wiser voices to shore up my points. My editors pushed back and said they wanted to hear more from *me*.

In other moments, I watch the thief killing my personality, hissing that I'm too much and that I need to hold back on who I am. As I auditioned to serve as cohost for a national radio ministry of Bible study, I self-edited, wondering if my personality would be too much for such a traditional platform. In the postaudition evaluation, I was asked to give *more* of my personality.

In still other instances, I observe the thief destroying my initiative to bring forth ideas, vision, and strategy. Sitting in a meeting, I bite my tongue from offering an opinion until it finally bursts forth in spoken words. Afterward, I wrestle with an internal accusation that I've said too much. To my surprise, a teammate applauds my contribution and underlines its helpfulness.

I look back over my life, from my little girl voice, to my prepubescent vessel, to my ever-emerging womb, to my scar story, to my grown-woman sway, and I hear the *Hissssss* that empties in each of these places. Like a helium balloon popped and whizzing air out across the room to collapse on the carpet. Like a cracked vase oozing water to the floor, leaving the flowers to wilt in dryness. Like a zero balance in a checking account well before the month's end.

The thief comes to steal, kill, and destroy the very fullness that Jesus came to give.

And you? Where has a thief stolen your fullness by poking a hole in your relationship with Jesus, leaking out all he longs to offer you? Where has a thief killed your hope, destroyed your day? We need to put in a security system against such a crook!

Here's the good news: we have the *best* security system possible. We have access to Jesus at every moment of every day and night. Jesus fills us with himself as we open our Bibles and read—and then he fills us again as he reminds us of what we've read, bringing a verse back to our minds later in the day or week. Journaling reminds us of how he has answered prayers when we tend to forget. Gathering with believers in the community of church and listening as others share about God's actions in their lives gives evidence of his work in our world.

Jesus is waiting to fill us—each of us—all of us—with himself. And he does this so personally! I love a good Matt Redman album in my ears as I plunge along the now-golden pathway with the view of the Rockies out behind my home, Jesus right at my side. Some are refilled in a relationship with God as they meander through an art gallery. Others receive filling as they serve a meal or tutor a child.

My friend Debbie sent me a photo she took while on a recent beach trip. The message she found written on the wooden wall of a bathroom on an old fishing pier was more than just initials inside a heart. Scrawled with a thick, black Sharpie were these words: "ALERT: Remember you are beautiful." It was signed, "Kisses, A." Debbie didn't know the identity of "A," but to her it might as well have been signed "Almighty God." She snapped the picture, texted it to me, and asked me if I thought God was into graffiti.

Don't you love that? God graffiti! The phrase made me stop and wonder just how often God scrawls such love into my everyday. And do I notice, or believe and receive? Not just a sip but to the brim—to *full*? Do you?

How does God fill you? Deal with the thief. Respond to Jesus' offer. Why settle for empty when Jesus came to give life to the full, to the *beauty full*?

Empty versus full. What a contrast!

Empty: a life that is stolen.

Full: a life that is saved.

Empty: a life alone.

Full: a life in relationship.

Empty: a life robbed of its potential.

Full: a life maximized.

Once we're filled to full, we are to spill! Tip! Slosh! Drip! Trickle, dribble, splatter—live life to the brim and *more*! When we live life to the full, others around us "want what we're having"!

Giving ourselves permission to see ourselves the way God does is so powerful (power *full!*). For ourselves—absolutely— but also deeply powerful for others, those who are watching us. "Legacy" is Dove's follow-up video to their Real Beauty Campaign, which I mentioned as we began our journey in the introduction. In this new film, women discover how their view of themselves affects their daughters' understandings of their own beauty—sometimes helping, sometimes hindering. One woman comments, "Self-worth and beauty—it is an echo—it can echo from me to them and then from them to others."[3]

Oh, so true! A contagious echo! A crescendo of convincing! That's what God's fullness in us accomplishes. God wants to fill you, that through you he might show others what they, too, can have in him. It's not up to us to run to fill up others. No, that's God's job. But we can be messy followers of Christ, our fullness revealing God's provision.

Musing over her preteen's morphing into womanhood, Alexandra Kuykendall splashed in clarity: "Could it be that the best way to show my girl with her long legs that she is valuable is for me to live a beautiful Jesus-obsessed life in front of her?"[4] Yes! Exactly. Not to shore up her every crack of insecurity with a mother's praise. Not to dress her in the latest and pretend her clothes will protect her. Not to pour out the very oil she herself needs as a mother in order to make it through the day. Rather, to model a Jesus-obsessed life where she can't move from point A to point B without the help of Jesus.

Sweet friend, we've journeyed so far together! We've honestly— sometimes *rawly*—considered together how God sees us and the zillion reasons we dismiss his view of us as possibly being real.

It's time to stop. And not just after *Hello, Beauty* and before *Full*. It's time to stop the ongoing Hiss that slithers through the *full*-fillment of what God is desperately trying to accomplish in us, of why he gave his Son to make sure we understand his love for and his view of us.

God sees us—you and me—as *beauty full*. To the brim! Not just pretty. Not just cute. Not just attractive. Not just part full or half full—but *full* full! It's time to stop settling for a sip. Jesus came to give us life to the brim and more!

One morning I pulled back the covers, shook the previous night's melatonin from my mind, and padded toward coffee. I shouted out to Jesus for strength and hope for my day, ran a few errands, and headed to my daughter's house, where I had promised to cover for several hours during Thanksgiving break. I had planned to take my ten-year-old grandson and his friend to Red Robin to get them out of the house and unplugged from technology for at least part of their day.

We piled in the car and drove the distance. As we walked to the entrance, the wind bit my body, and I zipped my magenta parka vest closed over my sweatshirt. I pulled my swirling hair from my eyes. Once through the heavy doors, we were greeted by a beaming hostess, who welcomed us with menus. Such enthusiasm! What was she, fifteen? I hitched up my sweatpants and traipsed after the girl, aware of her youthful energy, her glow, her packaged happiness—and my own windblown, underdressed state. As she led us through the maze of tables, she tossed questions to me over her shoulder: "All ready for Thanksgiving?" "Do you do anything special to celebrate?" When I answered, she turned her head just enough to catch my eye and smile in response. She was actually listening.

We slid into the appointed booth, and the hostess continued her banter about the upcoming holiday and then turned
our attention to some new techno game thingy installed in the
booth. The boys' eyes widened with anticipation of new buttons
and swipes and screens.

Then the girl paused—a bit longer than normal—and asked,
"May I tell you something?" Sincerity and intentionality creased
her young face.

"Of course." I said, ready for some bubbly recitation of food
options.

"You are very beautiful."

The boys looked up at me from their techno game thingy. My
grandson's friend, who didn't know me, squinted a bit. Marcus
stared and smiled.

I wondered, was this a marketing gimmick of Red Robin?
Were all hostesses now drilled to converse and compliment? Or
was this young girl doing a pay-it-forward kind of investment
on this Thanksgiving week? Maybe there was a competition at
school for who could say something nice most often. Possibly she
was a follower of Christ who had just studied a passage pushing
application the night before at her small-group Bible study.

Or maybe this girl was Jesus with skin on, reminding me yet
again that even here in the daily, *all* the time, he loves me and
sees me as beauty full. A God graffiti moment meant just for me.

The thief hissed, *"She doesn't mean* you*!"*

And then a whistling biker whizzed through my thoughts.
"Hello, beautiful." I paused, receiving the words from my Creator
who made me—voice, vessel, womb, scar, and sway—and *sees*

me. I moved my mind around to view myself the way God views me. I respelled the words of this young hostess in my mind as God spells them about me: *beauty full.*

With sincerity and intentionality, I locked eyes with her and said, "So are you: *beauty full.* So are you!"

Pause for just a second, will you? Lock your gaze on Jesus and take a breath. Hush that Hiss. See what God sees.

You: Beauty Full.

Becoming Beauty Full You

1. "I'm Enough!"
The band named "The Mrs." has taken on the challenge of creating music to help women of all ages embrace their enoughness and beauty. Founder Andra Liemandt and her bandmates recorded "I'm Enough" and created a video experience to help women see their beauty outside and in. Take a moment to listen to the song and watch the video for yourself at http://www.wimp.com/shelooked/.

2. Assess Your Symptoms: Empty to Full
From time to time, we're wise to give careful attention to current capacity. Are you full or running on empty or somewhere in between? Here are some questions to consider:

- Emotional
  Are you able to laugh at things that are really funny? Cry over the truly sad? Do you move along smoothly or roller-coaster between highs and lows?

Avoiding extremes and legitimately experiencing our emotions can be signs of emotional balance and restedness. The opposite? The gauge may be signaling low on reserves.

- Interpersonal

  How are your friendships—your marriage—your relationships with those most important to you? Interesting or boring? Competitive or collaborative? Revealing and honest or selective in sharing? Confrontational or clinging only to safe ground?

  Impatience, apathy, annoying resistance—negative actions and reactions can signal it's time to refuel your own tank.

- Physical Energy

  How is your appetite? Sleep pattern? Agility? Listen to what your body is saying about what this "temple of the Holy Spirit" might be asking for to continue thriving.

- Spiritual Zeal

  Does God seem close or far away to you? Is your first impression of yourself positive or negative, loved or unloved? Are you *ought*ing and *should*ing more than desiring and longing?

3. How Does God Fill You with Himself?

In his book *Sacred Pathways*, Gary Thomas outlines seven ways we can connect with God. Do you know your preferences? How does God reach out to fill you? How can you receive through the pathway he has created you to enjoy?

- Naturalists: Loving God out of doors
- Sensates: Loving God with the senses
- Traditionalists: Loving God through ritual and symbol
- Ascetics: Loving God in solitude and simplicity
- Activists: Loving God through confrontation
- Caregivers: Loving God by loving others
- Enthusiasts: Loving God with mystery and celebration
- Contemplatives: Loving God through adoration
- Intellectuals: Loving God with the mind[5]

4. How Do People Fill You, and How Do You Fill Them?
Do you know how you most enjoy loving others and receiving love from them? The full-circle reality of being loved by Jesus and then loving others from this fullness is strengthened when we understand how we, and significant people in our lives, speak love. Check out the five languages identified by Gary Chapman:

- Words of affirmation
- Acts of service
- Receiving gifts
- Quality time
- Physical touch[6]

5. A Full Exploration

There are endless elements of application for the concept of *Hello, Beauty Full.* Respond to the list below, and add your own ideas. How is God inviting you to apply the "see yourself how God sees you" concept in even more areas of your life?

- *Hello,* Power *Full*
- *Hello,* Grace *Full*
- *Hello,* Mercy *Full*
- *Hello,* Faith *Full*
- *Hello,* Care *Full*
- *Hello,* Wonder *Full*
- *Hello,* Joy *Full*
- *Hello,* _____ *Full*

PS—A WORD TO MOMS

I have a question for you: while reading this book, how many times did you think of your *beauty full* daughter? Or your daughter-in-law? Or your niece? Or maybe your best friend's daughter?

A lot?

I know. I thought of both my daughter and daughter-in-law throughout the writing. In fact, I dedicated this book to the two of them, because they have been behind my eyelids as I look at my keyboard and type.

But there can be a problem with this viewpoint, focusing on beauty for our daughters. When we look at them, we can forget to look at ourselves.

And then we teach them to do the same by our example. When we point out their beauty over and over and forget our own, they can actually forget their own as well. As Dove's follow-up survey, *Legacy*, reported, how we see ourselves influences how our daughters see themselves.[1] Eventually they, too, look around for some other reflection of who they might be, of how they might look, of how valuable they might be. They forget to look through the lens of who God sees them to be through Jesus.

Here's how to help your daughter know she is beautiful: *believe that you are beauty full.*

You may need to read this book again. That's fine. You're worth it. Turn back to the beginning and open the cover one more time, this time with you and only you in mind.

When we see ourselves as God sees us through Jesus—*beauty full*—we teach others that they are *beauty full* as well.

ACKNOWLEDGMENTS

When I really listen to my life, I realize that the anonymous biker dude is surely not the only one who has whispered, *"Hello, Beauty Full"* to me over the years. God has used many, many dear voices to woo me toward his vision of me.

Thanks to the editorial team at W Publishing for investing sweat and love to help shape my concepts and spruce up my writing so that more readers might make better sense of what I feel called to share. Debbie Wickwire, you are a woman after my heart—Be You TiFul! (There—I had to get that spelling in somewhere in these pages!) Meaghan Porter, your brilliant mind and beyond-your-years maturity have made me and this book better than I ever imagined.

Thanks to Rick Christian and Bryan Norman for sliding into a sacred spot once occupied by Lee Hough. I know he smiles from heaven at you hearing me out and helping me move ahead to even more of "Elisa." Thanks, too, to Steve Brock for your tireless work in putting words to my offering. Really.

Alexandra Kuykendall, Karen Schelhaas, Jessie Minassian, Carol Kuykendall—thank you for reading early versions and for highlighting what was working and what was not.

Thanks to my Facebook friends who responded to anonymous surveys to help me understand how most of us feel and think about our beauty, and to Heather Shore for your research assistance.

And to the forces that have shaped me—Elisa. I thank each of you who have held up God's mirror to gently—and firmly at times—turn my chin to gaze within, shedding shame, embracing beauty. The Fabs. The Cougars. The Covenant Sisters. Neighbors. Friends from high school through midlife. Terry and Paige. Mary. Munna and Bop. Cathy and Kirby. Jeff and Andy and Lynda. Evan. Eva, Jason, Marcus, Malachi, and Dominic. Ethan and Hilary. I am so grateful for each of you in my life, helping me embrace God's whisper in my days, *"Hello, Beauty Full."*

Yes, I am. And you are too!

NOTES

Introduction: Hello, Beautiful!

1. "Dove Real Beauty Sketches," Dove, http://realbeautysketches .dove.us.
2. Dove, "Only Two Percent of Women Describe Themselves as Beautiful," news release, September 29, 2004, http://www .prnewswire.com/news-releases/only-two-percent-of-women -describe-themselves-as-beautiful-73980552.html.
3. Dove, "Dove Real Beauty Sketches," YouTube video, 3:00, posted by "doveunitedstates," April 14, 2013, https://www.youtube.com /watch?v=XpaOjMXyJGk. See also http://realbeautysketches .dove.us.
4. Laura Stampler, "How Dove's 'Real Beauty Sketches' Became the Most Viral Video Ad of All Time," *Business Insider*, May 22, 2013, http://www.businessinsider.com/how-doves-real-beauty -sketches-became-the-most-viral-ad-video-of-all-time-2013-5.
5. Ibid.
6. Results from survey conducted by author via SurveyMonkey, March 5, 2014, Q7.
7. Synovate, "Men: Beauty or Brawn, or Both?" http://www.market researchworld.net/index2.php?option=com_content&task=view &id=2381&pop=1&page=0&ltemid=77.
8. Denis Campbell, "Body Image Concerns More Men Than Women, Research Finds," *Guardian*, January 5, 2012,

http://www.theguardian.com/lifeandstyle/2012/jan/06/body-image
-concerns-men-more-than-women/print.
9. Brennan Manning, *The Ragamuffin Gospel* (Sisters, OR: Multnomah, 1990), 117.

Part 1: Hello

1. William Grimes, "Great 'Hello' Mystery Is Solved," *New York Times*, March 5, 1992, http://www.nytimes.com/1992/03/05/garden /great-hello-mystery-is-solved.html.
2. Allen Koenigsberg, "The First 'Hello!': Thomas Edison, the Phonograph and the Telephone—Part 2," Collector Café, https://web .archive.org/web/20020706031939/http://www.collectorcafe.com /article_archive.asp?article=800&id=1507.

Chapter 1: The Hiss

1. Pamela Reeve, *Deserts of the Heart: Finding God During the Dry Times* (Sisters, OR: Multnomah, 2000), 114.
2. Sally Lloyd-Jones, *The Jesus Storybook Bible: Every Story Whispers His Name* (Grand Rapids: Zondervan, 2007), 12.
3. Ibid., 22.
4. Ibid., 29–30.
5. John Lynch, Bruce McNicol, and Bill Thrall, *The Cure: What If God Isn't Who You Think He Is and Neither Are You* (San Clemente: CrossSection, 2011), 12.
6. Brennan Manning, *Abba's Child: The Cry of the Heart for Intimate Belonging* (Colorado Springs: NavPress, 1994), 22.
7. Brené Brown, *Daring Greatly: How the Courage to Be Vulnerable Transforms the Way We Live, Love, Parent, and Lead* (New York: Gotham Books, 2012), 12.
8. Jerry Sittser, *A Grace Revealed: How God Redeems the Story of Your Life* (Grand Rapids: Zondervan, 2012), 24.
9. Mark Salzman, *Lying Awake* (New York: Random House, 2000), Kindle ed., 180.

10. Julian of Norwich, *The Revelations of Divine Love* (New York: Penguin, 1966), 56.

11. Sarah Young, *Jesus Calling: Enjoying Peace in His Presence* (Nashville: Thomas Nelson, 2004), November 1.

12. Karen Schelhaas, "She Said, He Said," *FullFill*, Spring/Summer 2014, 12–13.

Chapter 2: Not Me!

1. Jennifer Dukes Lee, "You Are PreApproved," *(in)courage* (blog), April 9, 2014, http://www.incourage.me/2014/04/you-are-preapproved.html.

2. Mark Galli, "The Love Shack," *Christianity Today*, March 2013, 33, http://www.christianitytoday.com/ct/2013/march/love-shack.html.

3. Ibid., 34.

4. Matthew Henry, *Matthew Henry's Commentary on the Whole Bible: Complete and Unabridged in One Volume* (Peabody, MA: Hendrickson, 1994), 1786–87.

5. Ann Voskamp, "How the Hidden Dangers of Comparison Are Killing Us . . . (and Our Daughters): The Measuring Stick Principle," *A Holy Experience* (blog), November 6, 2013, http://www.aholy experience.com/2013/11/how-the-hidden-dangers-of-comparison -are-killing-us-and-our-daughters-the-measuring-stick-principle/.

6. David A. Zimmerman, "What I'm Editing: The Easy Burden of Pleasing God," *Strangely Dim* (InterVarsity Press blog), January 17, 2013, http://strangelydim.ivpress.com/2013/01/what_im_editing _the_easy_burde.php.

Chapter 3: Shedding Shame

1. Camira Powell, "70% of Women Feel Depressed After Looking at a Fashion Magazine for 3 Minutes," *Mic*, July 11, 2012, http:// www.policymic.com/articles/10903/70-of-women-feel-depressed -after-looking-at-a-fashion-magazine-for-3-minutes.

2. Brené Brown, "Listening to Shame," TED 2012, March 2, 2012, Long Beach Performing Arts Center, Long Beach, CA, transcript

and video, 15:32, http://www.ted.com/talks/brene_brown_listening
_to_shame?language=en.

3. John Lynch, Bruce McNicol, and Bill Thrall, *The Cure: What If God Isn't Who You Think He Is and Neither Are You* (San Clemente: CrossSection, 2011), 30.

4. Stephen Tompkins, modernized and abridged version of St. Bernard of Clairvaux, *On Loving God,* https://www.christian historyinstitute.org/study/module/bernard/. The original text can be found at http://www.ccel.org/ccel/bernard/loving_god.i .html (see chapts. 8–10).

5. Rueben P. Job, *Three Simple Questions: Knowing the God of Love, Hope, and Purpose* (Nashville: Abingdon, 2011), Kindle ed., loc. 418.

6. Mandy Arioto, "Love Letter to Myself," *Mandy Arioto* (blog), September 13, 2010, http://www.mandyarioto.com/2010/09/love -letter-to-myself.html.

Chapter 4: Living Loved

1. Heidi McLaughlin, *Beauty Unleashed: Transforming a Woman's Soul* (Sisters, OR: VMI Publishers, 2007), 9.

2. Sharon Wegscheider Cruse, *Another Chance: Hope and Help for the Alcoholic Family,* 2nd ed. (Palo Alto, CA: Science and Behavior Books), 1989.

3. Henri Nouwen, *The Return of the Prodigal Son: A Story of Homecoming* (Doubleday, NY: Image Books, 1994), 106.

4. Ibid., 106–7.

5. Ibid., 107.

6. John Nolland, *The Gospel of Matthew, New International Greek Testament Commentary* (Grand Rapids: Wm. B. Eerdmans, 2005), 156–58.

7. Philip Yancey, *The Jesus I Never Knew* (Grand Rapids: Zondervan, 1995), 269.

8. Response to survey conducted by author via SurveyMonkey, March 5, 2014, Q3.

Part 2: Beauty

1. Edmund Burke, *On the Sublime and Beautiful*, vol. 24, pt. 2, The Harvard Classics (New York: P. F. Collier and Son, 1909–14); repr. Bartleby.com, 2001, http://www.bartleby.com/24/2/312.html.
2. Elizabeth Landau, "Beholding Beauty: How It's Been Studied," *CNN.com*, March 3, 2012, http://www.cnn.com/2012/03/02/health /mental-health/beauty-brain-research/.
3. Crispin Sartwell, *Six Names of Beauty* (New York: Routledge, 2004).
4. Thomas Aquinas, *Summa Theologica (13th c.)*, trans. Fathers of the English Dominican Province (London: Christian Classics, 1981), I, 39, 8.
5. Sartwell, *Six Names of Beauty*, vii.
6. Graham S. Ogden and Lynell Zogbo, *A Handbook on Ecclesiastes* (New York: United Bible Societies, 1998), 99.
7. David Hume, "Of the Standard of Taste," *Essays Moral and Political* (London: George Routledge and Sons, 1894), 136.

Chapter 5: Voice

1. Deborah Tannen, "Who Does the Talking Here?" *Washington Post*, July 15, 2007, http://www.washingtonpost.com/wp-dyn /content/article/2007/07/13/AR2007071301815.html.
2. Lesley Kinzel, "Mocking the US Women's Hockey Team for Crying over Their Loss to Canada Is Sexism, Pure and Simple," *XOJane*, February 21, 2014, http://www.xojane.com/sports/crying -olympic-hockey.
3. Carolyn Custis James, *Lost Women of the Bible: The Women We Thought We Knew* (Grand Rapids: Zondervan, 2005), 27–45.
4. Lisa Bevere, *Fight Like a Girl: The Power of Being a Woman* (New York: Warner Faith, 2006), 19.
5. National Center for Voice and Speech, "Voice Qualities," http:// www.ncvs.org/ncvs/tutorials/voiceprod/tutorial/quality.html.
6. John and Cindy Trent and Gary and Norma Smalley, *The Treasure Tree: Helping Kids Understand Their Personality* (Nashville: Tommy Nelson, 1992).

7. Gary Chapman, *The Five Love Languages: The Secret to Love That Lasts* (Chicago: Northfield Publishing, 1992).

8. Florence Littauer, *Personality Plus: How to Understand Others by Understanding Yourself* (Grand Rapids: Revell, 2001).

9. "MBTI Basics," The Myers & Briggs Foundation, http://www.myersbriggs.org/my-mbti-personality-type/mbti-basics.

10. Personality Profile Solutions, Inc., "DiSC Overview," DiscProfile, https://www.discprofile.com/what-is-disc/overview/.

11. Don Richard Riso and Russ Hudson, *The Wisdom of the Enneagram: The Complete Guide to Psychological and Spiritual Growth for the Nine Personality Types* (New York: Bantam Books, 1999).

12. Jeff Carver, "About Us," SpiritualGiftsTest.com, http://www.spiritualgiftstest.com/about-us.

13. Stephen Zades and Jane Stephens, *Mad Dogs, Dreamers and Sages: Growth in the Age of Ideas* (New York: Elounda, 2003), 91–92.

14. Richard Rohr, *Falling Upward: A Spirituality for the Two Halves of Life* (San Francisco: Jossey-Bass, 2011), iBook, 39.

15. Earl Creps, *Off-Road Disciplines: Spiritual Adventures of Missional Leaders* (San Francisco: Jossey-Bass, 2006), 14.

16. Simon Tugwell, *The Beatitudes: Soundings in Christian Tradition* (Springfield, IL: Templegate Publishers, 1980), 130.

17. Parker J. Palmer, *Let Your Life Speak: Listening for the Voice of Vocation* (San Francisco: Jossey-Bass, 2000), 16.

18. Nancy Beach, *Gifted to Lead: The Art of Leading as a Woman in the Church* (Grand Rapids: Zondervan, 2008), 120–28.

19. Anita Lustrea, *What Women Tell Me: Finding Freedom from the Secrets We Keep* (Grand Rapids: Zondervan, 2010), 170–71.

Chapter 6: Vessel

1. Marketing copy for Heidi McLaughlin, *Beauty Unleashed: Transforming a Woman's Soul* (Sisters, OR: VMI Publishers, 2007), http://www.amazon.com/Beauty-Unleashed-Transforming-Womans-Soul/dp/1933204400/ref=sr_1_sc_1?ie=UTF8&qid=1408369966&sr=8-1-spell&keywords=beauty+unleashed+heigh+mcLaughlin.

2. Galia Slayen, "The Scar8y Reality of a Real-Life Barbie Doll," *Huffington Post*, June 8, 2011, http://www.huffingtonpost.com /galia-slayen/the-scary-reality-of-a-re_b_845239.html.

3. Shaun Dreisbach, "Shocking Body-Image News: 97% of Women Will Be Cruel to Their Bodies Today," *Glamour*, http://www .glamour.com/health-fitness/2011/02/shocking-body-image -news-97-percent-of-women-will-be-cruel-to-their-bodies -today.

4. Carolyn Coker Ross, "Why Do Women Hate Their Bodies?" PsychCentral, http://psychcentral.com/blog/archives/2012/06/02 /why-do-women-hate-their-bodies/.

5. Ibid.

6. Results from survey conducted by author via SurveyMonkey, April 29, 2014, Q4.

7. "Uganda," *Jessica Simpson's The Price of Beauty*, episode 104, April 6, 2010, VH1.

8. "Paris," *Jessica Simpson's The Price of Beauty*, episode 102, March 23, 2010, VH1.

9. "Thailand," *Jessica Simpson's The Price of Beauty*, episode 101, March 12, 2010, VH1.

10. "Tokyo," *Jessica Simpson's The Price of Beauty*, episode 106, April 20, 2010, VH1.

11. Emma Barker, "These 26 Photos Show There's No One Way to Be Beautiful," *Elle*, June 25, 2014, http://www.elle.com/news/beauty -makeup/photoshop-beauty-standards.

12. Ashley Perez, "I Wasn't Beautiful Enough to Live in South Korea," Buzzfeed, May 31, 2013, http://www.buzzfeed.com/ashleyperez /i-wasn't-beautiful-enough-to-live-in-south-korea#.asQrdZRdN.

13. Ross, "Why Do Women Hate Their Bodies?"

14. Ibid.

15. Antoinette Y. Coulton and Julie Jordan, "World's Most Beautiful: Lupita Nyong'o," *People*, May 5, 2014, 74, http://www.people.com /people/article/0,20809897,00.html.

16. Ibid.

17. Results from survey conducted by author via SurveyMonkey, March 5, 2014, Q8.
18. Ibid., Q9.
19. Dreisbach, "Shocking Body-Image News."
20. Anne Lamott, *Traveling Mercies: Some Thoughts on Faith* (New York: Pantheon Books, 1999), 202.
21. Emily Wierenga, "Redefining the F-Word," *Hello, Darling* (blog), August 3, 2014, http://www.mops.org/blog/redefining-the-f-word.
22. Cynthia L. Ogden, Margaret D. Carroll, Brian K. Kit, and Katherine M. Flegal, "Prevalence of Obesity in the United States, 2009–2010," NCHS Data Brief, 82, January 2012.
23. Val Monroe, "Are You Ruining Your Sex Life?" *O, The Oprah Magazine*, October 2001, http://www.oprah.com/relationships /Self-Consciousness-During-Sex-Improving-Body-Image.
24. Susan Donaldson James, "Plus Model Elly Mayday Continues to Pose Despite Bald Head, Scars," ABC News, January 21, 2014, http://abcnews.go.com/Health/model-elly-mayday-fights-cancer -female-stereotypes/story?id=21597235.
25. Dan Allender and Tremper Longman III, *God Loves Sex: An Honest Conversation About Sexual Desire and Holiness* (Grand Rapids: Baker Books, 2014).
26. Pauline Rose Clance and Susan Imes, "The Imposter Phenomenon in High Achieving Women: Dynamics and Therapeutic Intervention," *Psychotherapy Theory, Research and Practice* 15:3, fall 1978, http:// www.paulineroseclance.com/pdf/ip_high_achieving_women.pdf.
27. Carrie Gann, "Women Beat Men on IQ Tests for First Time," ABC News, July 16, 2012, http://abcnews.go.com/blogs/health /2012/07/16/women-beat-men-on-iq-tests-for-first-time/.
28. John Naish, "Men's and Women's Brains: The Truth! As Research Proves the Sexes' Brains ARE Wired Differently, Why Women's Are Cleverer Ounce for Ounce—and Men Can't Read Female Feelings" *DailyMail*, December 4, 2013, http://www.dailymail .co.uk/femail/article-2518327/Mens-womens-brains-truth-As

-research-proves-sexes-brains-ARE-wired-differently-womens
-cleverer-ounce-ounce—men-read-female-feelings.html#ixzz3
HvfxBAbm.

29. Buckholdt Associates, "Men and Women Have Different Kinds
of Emotional Intelligence, High EQ for Both Sexes Is Key to
Workplace Success," Training Zone, http://www.trainingzone
.co.uk/partners/press/men-and-women-have-different-kinds
-emotional-intelligence-high-eq-both-sexes-key-work.

30. Raha Lewis, "Naked at 34," *People*, May 5, 2014, 103, http://www
.people.com/people/archive/article/0,20810156,00.html.

31. Kate Fox, "Mirror Mirror: A Summary of Research Findings on
Body Image," SIRC (Social Issues Research Centre), 1997, http://
www.sirc.org/publik/mirror.html.

32. H. D. M. Spence-Jones, ed., *I Corinthians* (New York: Funk &
Wagnalls, 1909), 194–95.

33. Barbara Brown Taylor, *An Altar in the World: A Geography of Faith*
(New York: HarperOne, 2009), 40.

34. Sarah Young, *Jesus Calling: Enjoying Peace in His Presence*
(Nashville: Thomas Nelson, 2004), November 7.

35. Results from survey conducted by author via SurveyMonkey,
April 29, 2014, Q10.

36. Taylor, *An Altar in the World*, 38.

37. Henri Nouwen, *The Inner Voice of Love: A Journey Through
Anguish to Freedom* (New York: Doubleday, 1996), 19; bracketed
material added by author.

38. Margot Starbuck, *Unsqueezed: Springing Free From Skinny Jeans,
Nose Jobs, Highlights, and Stilettos* (Downers Grove, IL: IVP
Books, 2010), 51.

39. Alexandra Kuykendall, "5 Ways to Let Girls Know They Are
Beautiful," *Alexandra Kuykendall.com* (blog), October 20, 2014,
http://alexandrakuykendall.com/alex/2014/10/20/5-ways-to-let
-girls-know-they-are-beautiful/.

40. Taylor, *An Altar in the World*, 38.

Chapter 7: Womb

1. Naomi Wolf, *The Beauty Myth: How Images of Beauty Are Used Against Women* (New York: Harper Collins, 2002), Kindle ed., 222.

2. Malin Rising and Maria Cheng, "Swedish Doctors Transplant Wombs into 9 Women," *Denver Post*, January 13, 2014, http://www.denverpost.com/breakingnews/ci_24899558/swedish-doctors-transplant-wombs-into-9-women.

3. Response from survey conducted by author via SurveyMonkey, April 29, 2014, Q9.

4. Emily T. Wierenga, "Redefining the F-Word," *Hello, Darling* (blog), August 3, 2014, http://www.mops.org/blog/redefining-the-f-word.

5. Jayne Spear, "Being a Home," *Hello, Darling*, Summer 2014, 26.

6. Parker J. Palmer, *Let Your Life Speak: Listening for the Voice of Vocation* (San Francisco: Jossey-Bass, 2000), 10.

7. Steven Garber, quoted in Kate Harris, *Wonder Women: Navigating the Challenges of Motherhood, Career, and Identity* (Grand Rapids: Zondervan, 2013), 26.

8. Barbara Brown Taylor, *An Altar in the World: A Geography of Faith* (New York: HarperOne, 2009), 110.

9. Frederick Buechner, *Wishful Thinking: A Theological ABC* (New York: Harper and Row, 1973), 95.

10. Palmer, *Let Your Life Speak*, 25.

11. Richard Rohr, *Falling Upward: A Spirituality for the Two Halves of Life* (San Francisco: Jossey-Bass, 2011), iBook, 34.

12. Jacky Gatliff, *FullFill* webinar, September 25, 2014.

13. Emily Perl Kingsley, "Welcome to Holland" (1987); reprinted in Pamela Bartram, *Understanding Your Young Child with Special Needs* (Philadelphia: Jessica Kingsley, 2007), 70–71.

14. Paulo Coelho, *The Alchemist* (New York: HarperCollins, 1993), 125.

Chapter 8: Scar

1. Amy Bloom, "Dear Every Woman I Know, Including Me," *O, The Oprah Magazine*, November 2011, http://www.oprah.com/spirit

/Improving-Body-Image-How-to-Feel-Beautiful-Improving-Self
-Esteem.

2. Karen Walrond, *The Beauty of Different: Observations of a Confident Misfit* (Houston: Bright Sky, 2010), foreword.

3. Walrond, "Karen Walrond at TEDxHouston 2012 Resonate," YouTube video, 15:14, from a presentation at TEDxHouston, November 3, 2012, https://www.youtube.com/watch?v=sau CsC9XUxY. The relevant section begins at 0:33.

4. Ibid. The relevant section begins at 10:47.

5. Camryn Berry, "See Beautiful Girl of the Month: Camryn Berry," *See Beautiful* (blog), April 21, 2014, http://seeabeautifulworld .blogspot.com/2014/04/see-beautiful-girl-of-month-camryn-berry .html.

6. Elisa Morgan, *The Beauty of Broken: My Story, and Likely Yours Too* (Nashville: W Publishing Group, 2013).

7. Victor Frankl, Harold S. Kushner, and William J. Winslade, *Man's Search for Meaning* (Boston: Beacon, 2006), iBooks, 320.

8. Brandon Appelhans and Stephen Albi, "Suffering Redeemed: Finding Purpose in the Pain of Mental Disorder," *Engage*, Fall 2013, 17, http://denverseminary.uberflip.com/i/199485/16.

9. D. A. Carson, *The Gospel According to John* (Grand Rapids: Eardmans, 1991), 656.

10. Sarah Young, *Jesus Calling: Enjoying Peace in His Presence* (Nashville: Thomas Nelson, 2004), August 20.

11. Dr. Frederick Field "Fritz" Ritsch III, "The Wounds of the Holy Spirit," sermon, St. Stephen Presbyterian Church, Fort Worth, TX, May 22, 2013, http://ststephen-pcusa.com/22–05–2013 /the-wounds-of-the-holy-spirit.

12. Steve Wiens, "Your Identity Is Not Equivalent to Your Biography," *The Actual Pastor* (blog), January 23, 2014, http://www.stevewiens .com/2014/01/23/your-identity-is-not-equivalent-to-your-biography/.

13. Henri Nouwen, *The Inner Voice of Love: A Journey Through Anguish to Freedom* (New York: Doubleday, 1996), 34–35.

14. Summarized from M. R. DeHaan, *Broken Things: Why We Suffer* (Grand Rapids: Discovery House, 1948), in Elisa Morgan, *The Beauty of Broken* (Nashville: W Publishing Group, 2013), 196–97.

Chapter 9: Sway

1. Sarah Young, *Jesus Calling: Enjoying Peace in His Presence* (Nashville: Thomas Nelson, 2004), June 6.
2. Parker J. Palmer, *Let Your Life Speak: Listening for the Voice of Vocation* (San Francisco: Jossey-Bass, 2000), 74.
3. Judith Couchman, *Designing a Woman's Life: Discovering Your Unique Purpose and Passion* (Sisters, OR: Multnomah, 1995), 136.
4. Sheryl Sandberg, *Lean In: Women, Work, and the Will to Lead* (New York: Knopf, 2013), 24.
5. John Ortberg, "What the Bible Says About Men and Women," July 7, 1999, #C9927, 2–3.
6. Catalyst, "Targeting Inequity: The Gender Gap in U.S. Corporate Leadership," September 28, 2010, http://www.jec.senate.gov/public /index.cfm?a=Files.Serve&File_id=90f0aade-d9f5–43e7–8501 –46bbd1c69bb8.
7. Lois P. Frankel, *See Jane Lead: 99 Ways for Women to Take Charge at Work* (New York: Hachette, 2007), 6.
8. Shauna Niequist, "What My Mother Taught Me," YouTube video, 17:58, from a presentation at Q Nashville, Nashville, TN, posted by "QIdeas.org," May 9, 2014, https://www.youtube.com/watch ?v=dIzgyW95grc. Quote begins at 14:53.
9. Anne Lamott, *Grace (Eventually): Thoughts on Faith* (New York: Riverhead Books, 2007), 139.
10. From survey conducted by author via SurveyMonkey, April 29, 2014, Q7.
11. Kelly Corrigan, *The Middle Place* (New York: Hyperion, 2008), 260.
12. Halee Gray Scott, *Dare Mighty Things: Mapping the Challenges of Leadership for Christian Women* (Grand Rapids: Zondervan, 2013), 125.
13. Ibid.

14. Frankel, *See Jane Lead*, 5–6.

15. Elisa Morgan, *She Did What She Could: Five Words of Jesus That Will Change Your Life* (Chicago: Tyndale, 2009).

16. Alice Mathews, "Women and Church Leadership" (course lecture), available for purchase at https://christiancourses.com/courses/women-and-church-leadership/.

17. Deborah Newman, *A Woman's Search for Worth: Finding Fulfillment as the Woman God Intended You to Be* (Wheaton: Tyndale, 2002), 43–44.

18. Desi McAdam, "How to Kick Ass in a Man's World," *5280 Magazine*, December 2013, 81, http://www.5280.com/magazine/2013/11/colorado-woman?page=6%2C6.

19. Diane Paddison, *Work, Love, Pray: Practical Wisdom for Young Professional Christian Women* (Grand Rapids: Zondervan, 2011), 188–89.

Chapter 10: To the Brim—and More!

1. Mandy Arioto, "To My Daughters, With Love," *Hello, Darling*, Summer 2014, 29.

2. Parker J. Palmer, *Let Your Life Speak: Listening for the Voice of Vocation* (San Francisco: Jossey-Bass, 2000), 80–81.

3. Dove, "Dove: Legacy," YouTube video, 2:54, posted by "doveunitedstates," September 30, 2014, https://www.youtube.com/watch?v=Pqknd1ohhT4.

4. Alexandra Kuykendall, "Does She Know She's Beautiful?" *Weekly ReFill*, June 30, 2014.

5. Gary Thomas, *Sacred Pathways: Discover Your Soul's Path to God* (Grand Rapids: Zondervan, 2000).

6. Gary Chapman, *The Five Love Languages: The Secret to Love That Lasts* (Chicago: Northfield, 1992).

PS A Word to Moms

1. Dove, "Dove: Legacy," YouTube video, 2:54, posted by "doveunitedstates," September 30, 2014, https://www.youtube.com/watch?v=Pqknd1ohhT4.

ABOUT THE AUTHOR

Elisa Morgan was named by *Christianity Today* as one of the top fifty women influencing today's church and culture and is one of today's most sought-after authors, speakers, and leaders. She has authored twenty-five books on mothering, spiritual formation, and evangelism, including *The Beauty of Broken, She Did What She Could,* and *The NIV Mom's Devotional Bible.*

For twenty years, Elisa Morgan served as CEO of MOPS International (www.mops.org). Under her leadership MOPS grew from 350 to more than 4,000 groups throughout the United States and in thirty other countries, influencing more than 100,000 moms every year. Elisa now serves as president emerita.

Elisa received a BS from the University of Texas and an MDiv from Denver Seminary. She served as the dean of women of Western Bible College (now Colorado Christian University) and on the board of ECFA (Evangelical Council for Financial Accountability). Currently she serves on the board of Denver Seminary.

Elisa is a cohost of the syndicated radio program *Discover the Word* (www.discovertheword.org), a daily fifteen-minute real-time conversation around the written and living Word of God. She is married to Evan (senior vice president of global ministry efforts for Our Daily Bread Ministries) and has two grown children and two grandchildren who live near her in Denver, Colorado. Wilson and Darla, her two rottweilers, take her on walks in the open space behind her house.

Connect with Elisa at www.elisamorgan.com. Sign up for her blog, *Really*, at her website or by texting the word REALLY to 22828. Keep in touch with Elisa on Facebook at Elisa Morgan, and on Twitter: @elisa_morgan.

Consider using *Hello, Beauty Full* for your small group or Bible Study. Discussion questions, devotions, and videos are available at elisamorgan.com.

Find beauty and hope by facing and dealing with the messiness of family life.

There's no such thing as a *perfect* family.

The
BEAUTY
of BROKEN

My Story and Likely Yours Too

Elisa Morgan

Small group discussion questions and videos available at elisamorgan.com

The family is an imperfect institution. Broken people become broken parents who make broken families. But actually, broken is normal and exactly where God wants us.

In *The Beauty of Broken*, Elisa Morgan, one of today's most respected female Christian leaders, for the first time shares her very personal story of brokenness—from her first family of origin to the second, represented by her husband and two grown children.

"*The Beauty of Broken* defies categories and breaks new ground as a raw account of a family that has been through everything—and in the process learned just how amazing grace is."

—Philip Yancey
Best-selling author, *What's So Amazing About Grace?*

AVAILABLE WHEREVER BOOKS AND E-BOOKS ARE SOLD

Want more of what you've read here?

———

elisamorgan.com

———

Sign up to receive Elisa's blog

Follow Elisa
On Facebook, Elisa Morgan
On Twitter, @elisa_morgan

Listen to Elisa on Discover the Word

Book Elisa to speak for your event

Elisa Morgan

Really

Living really … Really living